"Does This Cookbook Make Me Look Fat?"
Healthy Recipes even HE will eat!
A low fat/low carb cookbook

By Rona Lewis
Renowned Chef and Celebrity Fitness Trainer

Contact info:
Rona Lewis-818-568-5616
www.doesthiscookbookmakemelookfat.com
rona@ronafitness.com

Photography by Robert Lane
www.lumenosity.com
Photography and Graphics by James Franklin
www.jamesfranklin.net
Clive Pyne Book Indexing
www.cpynebookindexing.com

Table of Contents

"Food is an important part of a balanced diet."
Fran Lebowitz

Forward   p. vii
Introduction   p. 1
Acknowledgements   p. 2
Guide to Cooking Techniques   p. 4
Equipment   p. 6
Clean up Tools   p. 7
Liquid and Dry Measurements   p. 8
Pantry List   p. 9
Superfoods and their Health Benefits/Herbs and Spices   p. 11
Foods with that Extra Punch   p. 15
Mood Boosting Foods   p. 18
The Best Time of the Year to Buy   p. 20
Explanation of Vitamins and Minerals   p. 21

Recipes
Breakfasts-   p. 25
    Deviled Crab Egg White Omelet   p. 26
    Egg, Mushroom & Roasted Red Pepper Burritos   p. 27
    Omelet with Summer Vegetables   p. 28
    Asparagus and Leek Frittata   p. 29
    Herbed Asparagus Omelet   p. 30
    Vegetable Breakfast Quiche   p. 31
    Power Muffins   p. 33
    Outrageous Oatmeal   p. 34

Salads-   p. 37
    Watercress and Orange Salad   p. 38
    Tomato and Zucchini Salad   p. 39
    Tomato and Sweet Pepper Salad   p. 40
    Moroccan Carrot Salad   p. 41
    Heirloom Tomato, Lime and Onion Salad   p. 42
    Grilled Eggplant Salad   p. 43
    Asian Slaw   p. 44
    Cherry Tomatoes with Watermelon   p. 45
    Tofu Salad   p. 46

Soups-   p. 49
    Wild Mushroom Stock   p. 50
    Tomato Soup with Roasted Peppers   p. 51
    Sweet Pepper Soup   p. 52
    Spicy Red Pepper Soup   p. 53

Spicy Kale Chowder with Chicken Sausage p. 54
Southwest Shrimp Soup p. 55
Onion Soup p. 56
Minestrone p. 57
Lentil Spinach Soup p. 58
Hot and Sour Soup p. 59
Gazpacho p. 60
Cucumber Mint Soup p. 61
Cold Cream of Cucumber Soup p. 62
Broccoli Soup p. 63
Chicken Florentine Soup p. 64
Mom's Garbage Soup p. 65

Side Dishes- p. 69
Stewed Beans with Kale p. 70
Zucchini and Carrots with Fresh Mint or Parsley p. 71
Yellow Tomatoes in Balsamic Vinaigrette p. 72
Roasted Red Peppers p. 73
Ratatouille p. 74
Oven-Baked Mixed Vegetables p. 75
Mushrooms in Lemon Marinade p. 76
Marinated Zucchini p. 77
Italian Pepper Saute p. 78
Haricot Verts with Garlic p. 79
Green Beans Provencal p. 80
Cherry Tomatoes with Garlic and Parsley p. 81
Broiled Tomatoes p. 82
Braised Mixed Bell Peppers p. 83
Garbanzos with Spinach p. 84

Main Courses- p. 87
Veal Stew with Tomatoes and Balsamic Vinegar p. 88
Casserole of Lamb and Eggplant p. 89
Boneless Loin of Lamb with Tarragon p. 90
Pork Chops Pizzaiola p. 91
Grilled Pork Medallions with Herb Marinade p. 92
Stir-Fried Pea Shoots and Shiitakes with Shrimp p. 93
Asian Style Foil Fish p. 94
Charcoal-Broiled Shrimp p. 95
Fish Fillets in Foil p. 96
Grilled Shrimp with Thai Lemongrass Marinade p. 97
Light Shrimp Scampi p. 98
Poached Salmon with Cucumber Sauce p. 99
Poached Trout p. 100
Shrimp in New Orleans Sauce p. 101
South of the Border Shrimp p. 102

Turkey for Pocket Sandwiches   p. 103
Oven Roasted Vegetables w Italian-Style Turkey Sausage   p. 104
Quick Italian Chili-1 skillet meal   p. 105
Turkey Chili   p. 106
Basic Sauté of Chicken and Herbs   p. 107
Chicken Breasts with Peppers   p. 108
Baked Chicken with Wild Rice   p. 109
Ratatouille with Chicken Sausage   p. 110
Oriental Grilled Chicken   p. 111
Chicken in Red Wine Sauce   p. 112
Chicken Pesto   p. 113
Chicken with Peppers   p. 114
Tequila Marinated Beef for Fajitas   p. 115
Ground Beef with Lebanese Spices   p. 116
Grilled Salmon and White Bean Salad   p. 117
Herb-Marinated Lamb Chops   p. 118
Marinated Skirt Steak   p. 119
Italian-Style Beef Burgers   p. 120
Pork Fajitas with Pan Roasted Peppers   p. 121
Spicy Tofu Stew   p. 122
Vegetarian Chili   p. 123
Lean Meatballs   p. 124

Sauces, Dips and Salsas-   p. 127
Roasted Red Pepper Tomato Sauce   p. 128
Fresh Mango Salsa   p. 129
Peach Salsa   p. 130
Basic Marinara Sauce   p. 131
Black Bean Confetti Relish   p. 132
Caramelized-Onion Sauce   p. 133
Eggplant and Garlic Dip   p. 134
Mutabbel   p. 135
Compuesta Dip   p. 136

Desserts-   p. 139
Apple Brown Betty   p. 140
Broiled Peaches and Strawberries   p. 141
Chocolate Cheesecake   p. 142
Chocolate Glazed Pears   p. 143
Summer Fruit Salad   p. 144
Apple Pie a la Mode Parfaits   p. 145
Creamy Ice Banana   p. 146

Fun and Easy Home Remedy Tips   p. 147
Quotes and Quips from my (so-called) Friends   p. 149
Index   p. 150

This page intentionally left blank

Forward

Bravissimo Rona!

My good friend, Rona, has written a brilliant cookbook filled with great recipes. You feel as though she is right there in the kitchen with you! This is one of those rare cookbooks that…if you can read the recipe…you can cook it. Rona's use of fresh ingredients makes your mouth water as you read each recipe. Her stories and anecdotes are so real and easy to relate to, you'll feel as though you have a spot at the family's table.

The purpose of this cookbook is to provide you with the tools to prepare tasty, healthy meals for you and your loved ones, as well as to bring back some quality family time to the kitchen table.

The recipes in this book are proof positive that healthy cooking is delicious, whether you are a novice or a professional in the kitchen. This book has a lesson for all.

Go ahead, prepare a few recipes, set the table, gather the family and unplug the TV-Fress a bissel (translation-Eat a little!)

Buy two-one to give to a friend and one to use in your kitchen daily.

BARRY WILLNER, OWNER   PRIZZI'S PIAZZA, HOLLYWOOD, CA.

"Half the cookbooks tell you how to cook the food, the other half tell you how to avoid eating it."

Andy Rooney

This page intentionally left blank

Introduction

"Health nuts are going to feel stupid someday, lying in hospitals dying of nothing."
Unknown, Explore magazine, 6/2007

I can't say that I was a child prodigy with food, making soufflés before I could walk, or that I was educated at the Cordon Bleu. I can, however, say that I've always been a big fan of food. My whole family has. My Mom is actually a great cook, which was directly proportional to the family's consumption of food. She always cooked for 8 and we only had a family of 5! There were never any leftovers...and none of us kids weighed over 100 pounds until we were in 11th grade (our metabolisms have all slowed significantly since that time)! Under these circumstances, it was difficult to get near the kitchen, so I never really learned how to cook until after graduating from **Penn State**. (I ate a LOT of sticky buns and Creamery ice cream, needless to say!) It was a necessity. Living on my own, I got tired of eating Cup O' Noodles, tuna with stewed tomatoes (don't knock it 'til you've tried it!) and the corner Korean salad bar. I started experimenting with easier recipes and found that, like my mother, I had that creative ability to make something yummy out of whatever was left in the 'fridge. That, combined with studying Pierre Franey's "60 Minute Gourmet" recipes every Wednesday in the New York Times, helped to make me a cook whose friends would actually want to come over for something to eat!

In the years that followed, working in the health and wellness industry made me very conscious of what I was putting into my body. My prowess as a cook enabled me to develop my own healthy recipes and re-engineer others' into healthier versions with a lot of taste. One of my greatest pleasures is cooking for my friends. Actually, it was their idea for me to do this. They kept telling me, "You should write a cookbook! You should really write a cookbook!"

"Alright already," I said. "Stop nagging! I'll write, I'll write."

So I did.

Not all of my recipes are super-duper low calorie, either. I realize that hypothetically, everything being equal...in a vacuum...we all want to eat perfectly well every day. BUT, as John Lennon said, "Life happens while you're planning other things." You have to live in this world and be prepared for anything; cook for unexpected company, manage to cook dinner for kids who won't eat it unless it's a carbohydrate or splurge on something decadent for yourself. ***Does This Cookbook Make Me Look Fat?*** *Healthy Recipes Even HE Will Eat!* allows readers to do all of these things—enjoy cooking and eating, not make it a chore, and for the most part, keep their bodies healthy. It also explains what makes the recipes healthy in a manner that is easy to understand.

I hope I can make your meals a little healthier and make you laugh while you prepare them. Enjoy!

"The highlight of my childhood was making my brother laugh so hard that food came out of his nose."
Garrison Keillor

Acknowledgments

"Cuisine is just fine, but there are times when food is better."
Unknown

When I think about my childhood, I remember my Mom always being in the kitchen. It's a ridiculous notion, as she was a successful interior designer who was also involved with the after school sports of all three of her kids, as well as being class mother, etc, etc, etc. But Mom was and is a great cook. She liked to call herself "a peasant cook." There were no puff pastries or cream sauces or escargot. (Although, I'm sure if she put her mind to it, and if it was Kosher, she could have whipped 'em up with no problem) Her dishes were straightforward, well seasoned and for the most part, pretty healthy. She insisted all of us sit down to dinner as a family, a notion that seems to be going by the wayside in today's world.

She always asked if I wanted to learn how to cook whatever she was serving that night. Most of the time I was too busy sitting in front of the TV or on the phone with my friends. But, as I got older, and was thinking about college and beyond, I started paying attention and now have a good base of standards from her in my repertoire. Some of those are included here. Thanks for those, Mom!!

When I started in the fitness business, a long time ago, I wanted to be a true resource for my clients. To me, that meant not only being an expert on how and when to exercise, but also being able to give my clients sound nutritional advice and ways to keep them on track. So, I gave them meal plans and suggested supplements, as well as recipes that were low fat, easy and delicious. Clients LOVED them. So, I started collecting recipes and modifying the ones that my pupils gave me that they enjoyed and didn't want to stop eating. I also learned about the healing and nutritional value of herbs and spices. After a while, my friends started "harassing me" to put this information together and write a cookbook, as the dishes I cook are so diverse and different. OK! Stop already! Here it is!

The majority of my clients and friends are women over 35 with kids, a job and not a lot of free time. They are my heroes. These women are smart, resourceful and able to squeeze 37 hours into a 24-hour day. I hope this book becomes a go-to item for them. Thanks to all of you for pushing me to do this.

To my friends who love to eat my food as much as I love to cook for them: You gave me great feedback on new recipes and my joy in cooking for you is only surpassed by the joy I feel in your company.

To Cathy Carlson. You saved my life and made me believe I can do anything. And I can.

To Julie Glick. We've gone through parallel experiences and come out ahead. You showed me how powerful I really am. You rock!

To Cathleen Tierney Finn. You never forgot how to be a best friend even when you were dealing with your own stuff. You're the sister I never had and I'm grateful for having you in my life.

2

To Margie Fisher. Zable Fisher Public Relations, Inc. is known all over the country and you were willing to help a friend who's just starting out. Your heart is as big as your client list!

To my big brother, Mark. Your sense of humor and rapier wit helped me make this book even better. Thanks not only for your editing help, but also for believing your little sister can do something else besides whine. You're right…I can always depend on you.

This book is dedicated to my Mom, who made me appreciate great food and to my Dad, the dentist, who made sure my teeth were healthy enough to eat it.

Rona Lewis

"The most remarkable thing about my mother is that for 30 years she served the family nothing but leftovers. The original meal has never been found."

Calvin Trillin

Guide to Cooking Techniques

"She was so wild that when she made French toast she got her tongue caught in the toaster."
Rodney Dangerfield

Al Dente: Slightly underdone, chewy. Usually applied to pasta, but can be used to describe vegetables.

Baking: To cook in the oven using heated dry air. Make sure you pre-heat the oven before the food goes in.

Blanching: To plunge food into boiling water for a short period of time.

Boiling/Simmering: To heat water or other liquids to 212 degrees

Braising: To brown meat in fat over high heat, then cover and cook slowly in the oven in a small amount of liquid.

Broiling/Grilling: To cook with intense direct heat either on the grill or under a broiler. The high heat seals in the juices, which keeps the meat tender.

Dice: To cut into equal-sized small cubes around ½".

Dilute: To make a sauce or stock less strong flavored by adding more liquid

Drain: To remove liquid or fat from food through a strainer or by absorbing it with a paper towel.

Hull: To pluck out the stems and leaves of berries.

Julienne: To cut fresh vegetables or other foods into thin, matchstick strips.

Line: To cover the surface of a baking sheet or roasting pan with foil to prevent drips and sticking.

Marinate: To tenderize and flavor food by placing it in a seasoned liquid.

Microwaving: to heat or cook food or beverages using an oven that uses high-frequency electromagnetic radiation.

Pan-Broil: To cook on top of a stove in a preheated heavy skillet over high heat, pouring off fat and liquid as it accumulates.

Parboil: To partially cook in boiling water or broth. Often vegetables are parboiled and finished of by sautéing.

Pare: To remove skin or rind from fruits and vegetables using a thin knife.

Poach: To cook food gently in simmering liquid that does not boil. For best results, food should be started in warm liquid and then slowly brought to a simmer.

Pound: To flatten or tenderize meat, often between sheets of waxed paper, with a mallet or saucepan.

Preheat: To set an oven or broiler at the desired temperature 15 -20 minutes before use so that the desired temperature is reached before food is put in to cook.

Reduce: To thicken or concentrate a sauce by boiling down, which lessens the amount, but intensifies the flavor.

Roasting: To cook by the free circulation of dry heat, often beginning with a very hot oven to seal in juices and then lowering the heat to complete the cooking. Can also be done on a spit.

Sautéing: To cook food in butter or oil in a skillet until lightly browned.   Usually a quick process.

Sear: To brown the surface of meat very quickly in a hot oven, under a broiler or in a pan over high heat on top of the stove to seal in juices.

Simmer: To cook liquid alone or along with other ingredients over low heat, never boiling.

Steaming: To cook food, covered, over a small amount of boiling water or broth. This is the best way to cook low fat veggies.

Stir Frying: To quickly sauté meat or vegetables while stirring constantly in a hot wok or skillet.

"The only time to eat diet food is while you are waiting for the steak to cook."
Julia Child

Equipment

"You become about as exciting as your food blender. The kids come in look you in the eye, and ask if anybody's home."
Erma Bombeck

While it's not necessary to have a ton of items to prepare your dishes, these are the basics to make life easier and to cut down on preparation time.

Food Processor
Blender
Cutting Boards-Have 2 or 3 of different sizes. You don't always need a giant cutting area, so vary the size. I prefer the anti-bacterial ones I can throw in the dishwasher when I'm done.
Microwave
Bowls-A set of nesting bowls. My favorite set has 9 glass bowls and can be bought at Bed, Bath and Beyond or Linens and Things for about $15. Have a couple of stainless steel bowls on hand, as well.
Colanders
Knives of varying sizes for chopping, slicing, coring, etc.
Soup Pot
Large 4 or 5 quart skillet
8" omelet pan
Saucepans with lids
Timer with bell
Garlic Press
Baking pans
Roasting Pan with Rack
Kitchen Shears
Measuring Cups
Good pair of tongs
Immersion Blender-Stick Hand Blender
Stand Mixer
Zester/Grater
Salad Spinner

Cleanup Tools

"If you wish to make an apple pie truly from scratch, you must first invent the universe."
Carl Sagan (1934-1996), Cosmos

OK, you've cooked up a storm. If you're like me, you're not the neatest cook in the world. I hope you have everything you need to make cleaning up easy! Here's a list of essentials to help you get the job done quickly and easily. (Check the ceiling for splashes… you never know!)

Dishwashing liquid
Sink Strainer
Rubber Gloves
Dish Towels
Sink Mat (keeps glasses and dishes from chipping and breaking)
Dish Rack
Sponges
Special Cleaning Brushes for glassware

Optional: A Dog for what you've dropped on the floor.

"All I ask of food is that it doesn't harm me."
Michael Palin (Monty Python's Flying Circus)

Liquid and Dry Measurements

"A good cook is not necessarily a good woman with an even temper. Some allowance should be made for artistic temperament."
X. Marcel Boulestin , chef, food writer (1878-1943)

Dash=1/4 tsp
3 teaspoons = 1 tablespoon = ½ ounce (liquid and dry)
2 tablespoons = 1 oz (l and d)
4 tablespoons = 2 oz = ¼ cup
5 1/3 tablespoons = 1/3 Cup
32 tablespoons = 16 oz = 2cups = 1 pound
64 tablespoons = 32 oz = 1 quart = 2 pounds
1 cup = 8 oz = ½ pint
2 cups = 16 oz = 1 pint
4 cups = 32 oz = 2 pints = 1 quart
16 cups = 128 oz = 4 quarts = 1 gallon
1 quart = 2 pints

Then there's the kind I use, for those recipes that never come out the same twice:

Some= Shake it a few times for flavor or throw in about a handful.
Lots=Shake it until it covers whatever you're cooking or throw out the rest of the ingredients and just eat that.
A bunch=Similar to Lots, but with fresh ingredients, like herbs.

"We live in an age when pizza gets to your home before the police."
Jeff Arder

Pantry List

"Hunger: One of the few cravings that cannot be appeased with another solution."
Irwin Van Grove

The list below contains many of the ingredients in this book. Many, though, should be a staple in your cabinets, especially for last minute meals and surprise guests. Herbs, spices and condiments make any basic meal extra-special and tasty, without missing the extra oil, salt or fat. There are times you can experiment by substituting one herb for another…tarragon for basil, for instance. Be creative and you'll be pleasantly surprised. I'm assuming you have the super basic staples like onions, pepper and olive oil, so I'm giving you the benefit of the doubt.

Low sodium canned beans:
Black Beans
Red Kidney Beans
Garbanzo Beans

Nuts:
Almonds
Cashews
Pine Nuts
Sesame Seeds

Herbs and Spices:
Basil
Cayenne
Cilantro
Coriander
Cinnamon
Cumin
Curry powder
Dill
Garam Masala
Nutmeg
Oregano
Onion Powder
Paprika
Red Pepper Flakes
Rosemary
Saffron
Sage
Tarragon
Thyme
Tumeric

Miscellaneous:
Dried Mushrooms
Fresh Garlic
Sun-dried Tomatoes
Chili Oil

"Dieting: A system of starving yourself to death so you can live a little longer."
Jan Murray

Super foods and their Health Benefits

"This stuff tastes awful; I could have made a fortune selling it in my health-food store."
Woody Allen, 'Sleeper'

Herbs and Spices

Herbs and spices have been used for thousands of years to help fend off physical ailments and illnesses. Here is a list of some of the more popular ones:

Anise-Antifungal against Candida and is an antihistamine. Used by Native Americans to help with allergies and asthma. As a tea, it can relieve digestive disorders and cramps. It's useful to loosen phlegm and against coughs and colds.

Basil-Anti-inflammatory and antibacterial. Helps to reduce stomach cramps and nausea, relieves gas and can promote normal bowel functions.

Cardamom-Can soothe indigestion, ease congestion and kill bad breath. Try grinding it and sprinkling on top of an herbal tea. This boosts energy yet prevents insomnia.

Caraway-The seeds from this plant can be considered an herb when used for flavoring. Caraway is soothing for gas and other stomach disorders and when brewed into a tea is excellent for coughs and colds.

Cayenne pepper and Tabasco sauce- Can increase metabolism and fat-burning ability by up to 25%. Cayenne stimulates the production of gastric juices and helps relieve gas. It also appears to have a beneficial impact on blood sugars.

Chamomile-Chamomile is used mostly for teas and has a calming effect on smooth muscle tissue. It works well for menstrual cramps and other stress related problems. When used as a mouthwash, chamomile can relieve the pain of a toothache!

Chives-High in Vitamin C and Iron, they are useful against anemia. Chives also stimulate the appetite and aid in digestion.

Cinnamon-Fights cancer, heart disease and helps diabetics decrease blood glucose. Also an antibacterial and antifungal as well as an anti-inflammatory. Cinnamon's other benefits include:
Supporting digestive function
Constricting and toning tissues
Relieving congestion
Relieving pain and stiffness of muscles and joints
Relieving menstrual discomfort

Has blood-thinning compounds that stimulate circulation
Has anti-inflammatory compounds that may relieve arthritis
Helping to prevent urinary tract infections, tooth decay and gum disease
It's also a powerful anti-microbial agent that can kill E. Coli and other bacteria

Cloves-Have a potent, sweet and spicy, aromatic flavor that make a great complement to many foods. They have been consumed in some areas, such as Asia, for more than 2,000 years. Among the clove's most well known healing properties is its ability to relieve tooth and gum pain, but it has many benefits beyond that. These include:

Anti-inflammatory, anti-bacterial and antioxidant properties
Relief from respiratory ailments such as asthma and bronchitis
Relief from muscle pains from injuries or arthritis and rheumatism
Eliminating intestinal parasites, fungi and bacteria
May encourage creativity and mental focus

Curry-Helps ward off cancer, heart disease and diabetes

Dill-Used often as a digestive aid and a remedy for a sour, gassy stomach. Chewing dill, like parsley, can cure bad breath.

Fennel-Fights stomach bloat and helps with gas. Fennel oil with honey in some warm water is a great age-old expectorant for coughs. Fennel tea is also good for the pancreas.

Flaxseed-These little guys have a ton of alpha-linoleic acid. This helps slow bone breakdown. One tablespoon gives you 1.6g of ALA. That's more than you'll need in one day! Cool, huh?

Garlic-This powerful plant may be the wonder drug of natural healing. Louis Pasteur discovered that garlic could kill microorganisms. Albert Schweitzer used garlic to treat cholera and other diseases while working as a missionary in Africa. It's an anticoagulant that helps reduce the risk of blood clots and helps to lower cholesterol while increasing the level of HDL (the good cholesterol). It fights cancer and heart disease by reducing blood pressure and blood lipids and helps fight infection.

Ginger-Helps with sore throats. Fights cancer and heart disease. It has a potent flavor that is great for warming your body and adding kick to foods. Its medicinal properties include:

Soothing nausea, motion sickness and other stomach upset
Relieving morning sickness
Having an anti-inflammatory property
Eliminating intestinal gas
Relaxing and soothing the intestinal tract
Having antioxidant properties

Relieving dizziness
Boosting the immune system
Protecting against bacteria and fungi
Encouraging bile flow
Promoting cardiovascular health

Holy Basil-No…not Holy Basil, Batman! Just holy basil. This is a special variety of basil that's effective at reducing stress by increasing adrenaline and noradrenaline and decreasing serotonin. The leaves also make a nifty tea that relieves indigestion and headaches. You can find this in any good health food store.

Horseradish-An excellent diuretic and is great for digestion. It's a good expectorant and helps with respiratory problems.

Hot peppers-Help fight cancer, heart disease and diabetes.

Lemon Juice-Prevents kidney stones. It contains citrate, an acid that binds to the crystals in the urine that can cause stones to grow.

Mustard- A stimulant that can be used to relieve respiratory complaints.

Nutmeg-It kills harmful bacteria in the GI tract. Has some antidepressant properties. Nutmeg is another spice that has a variety of healing properties and can be used in a wide range of dishes during the holidays and all year long. It is useful for:

Insomnia (nutmeg can produce drowsiness so it should be taken when you have a chance to relax or sleep)
Anxiety
Calming muscle spasms
Nausea and vomiting
Indigestion
Diarrhea
Joint pain and gout
Lowering blood pressure
Male infertility and impotence
Improving concentration
Increasing circulation
Lowering cholesterol
Toothaches (nutmeg oil)

Parsley- It's a natural antispasmodic, and is great for the digestion. It relieves gas and is a natural diuretic. Also, it's a great natural breath freshener.

Pepper-Fights cancer and heart disease

Peppermint-Smooth muscle relaxant and soothes IBS. Peppermint tea is a popular anti-gas, stomach settling drink after dinner. Peppermint's healing properties include:

Soothing to the digestive tract and it also helps with nausea and vomiting.
Relieves symptoms of irritable bowel syndrome
May protect against cancer
Inhibits the growth of bacteria and fungus
Relieves the symptoms of allergies and asthma

Rosemary-Fights cancer and heart disease. It's used to treat dizziness due to inner ear disturbances. Sipped as tea, it's been reputed to be good for nervous tension and is especially good if you have tension headaches. It can also help extract carcinogens that enter the body from binding with DNA, the first step in tumor formation.

Sage-Mild mood enhancer. Helps with sore throats and coughs and may help hot flashes. Also improves brain nourishment when brewed as a tea. The extract may help those with excessively sweaty palms.

Thyme-Antibacterial, antifungal and eases bronchitis and upper respiratory infections.

Turmeric- contains curcumin, an antioxidant. Turmeric is a strong immunomodulator. It prevents sickness, may help fight colon cancer and is an antioxidant and antimicrobial. Turmeric has a beneficial effect on the liver, stimulating the flow of bile and the breakdown of dietary fats.

"I feel the end approaching. Quick, bring me my dessert, coffee and liqueur."
Brillat-Savarin's Great Aunt Pierette

Foods with that Extra Punch!

"It is odd how all men develop the notion, as they grow older, that their mothers were wonderful cooks. I have yet to meet a man who will admit that his mother was a kitchen assassin and nearly poisoned him."

Robertson Davies, Canadian author (1913-1995)

Make sure you include plenty of these foods in your diet. They'll help everything from your skin to your eyesight to your bones. This is especially true if you don't take a multivitamin!

Almonds- Almonds are high in monounsaturated fats. Furthermore, almonds have many health-promoting minerals, especially magnesium, but also potassium, which means the nuts help other dietary and supplemental sources protect cardiovascular health. Eating almonds with their skins provides medically significant amounts of vitamin E and flavonoids. Almonds contain fiber are also a good source of protein (6 grams per ounce) almost the same amount as one egg (6.3 grams of protein/egg).

Avocados-Avocados are high in monosaturated fat. That's a healthy fat we need. They've got folate, magnesium, Vitamin E and are very high in lutein. And, one serving of avocado contains 12 grams of fiber! That's 33% more than a cup of shredded wheat cereal. They also increase the absorption of fat-soluble phytonutrients, such as lycopene, found in tomatoes. Dig into that guacamole!!

Blueberries-Rich in fiber, vitamin C and antioxidants. Extracts of blueberry (and strawberry!) may help protect the brain against age-related oxidative stress.

Black Beans- Black beans have more antioxidants than any other kind of bean and high amounts of folate, which helps reduce the risk of heart attacks. The fiber helps to lower cholesterol, regulate blood sugar and work towards preventing diabetes.

Broccoli-May help prevent age related macular degeneration.

Brussels Sprouts-These leafy greens are high in vitamin K, which helps bone retain calcium. Many early post-menopausal women don't get enough of this vitamin.

Chocolate-Dark chocolate is high in flavonol, an antioxidant that moderately reduces cholesterol and improves circulation. Keep it to about ½ ounce, though. Those calories can add up.

Figs-Figs have more calcium than almost any other fruit, about 15% of your daily needs.

Fish Oil-Taken as pills, combined with exercise can help promote weight loss in overweight people. It increases fat burning by improving blood flow to the muscles during exercise.

Flaxseed-The seeds must be ground in order to absorb the nutrients, but a little goes a long way. One tablespoon has as much fiber as a whole bowl of oatmeal. It's got a ton of manganese for building bone; and magnesium, good for the bones, muscles and nerves. Studies have shown that flaxseed can also reduce the growth of breast cancer tumors. These little guys have a ton of alpha-linolenic acid (ALA). This helps slow bone breakdown. One tablespoon gives you 1.6g of ALA. That's more than you'll need in one day! Cool, huh?

Green Tea-More and more studies are showing this tea's ability to reduce risk of cancer and the risk of coronary-artery disease as well as lowering cholesterol and blood pressure. Green tea is also noted in traditional Asian medicine as being an excellent blood purifier.

Pomegranates-This fruit's medicinal properties have been utilized in the Middle East for thousands of years. Not only is it a powerhouse of potassium, but research shows that a mere 8 oz. glass of its juice has about 3 times the antioxidants of red wine or green tea! It's also been known to ease menopausal symptoms, strengthen bones, combat heart disease and high blood pressure.

Sesame Seeds: Consuming sesame may promote healthy blood lipids. Helps post-menopausal women with cancer protection and estrogen metabolism.

Spinach-Spinach makes any salad into a vitamin packed meal. Or try it cooked, so the nutrients are more easily assimilated into the body. It's high in iron and antioxidants, like lutein for eyes. It's also high in vitamins, A, C and K.

Sweet Potatoes-Another antioxidant powerhouse, sweet potatoes have tons of fiber (eat the skin!), vitamin C and potassium. They have beta-carotene, which helps eyesight and protects you from infection.

Tomatoes-This fruit is known for its beta-carotene, vitamin C and lycopene. Lycopene absorbs more easily after it's been cooked, but the other tomato nutrients lose their power, so make sure you eat a combination of cooked and raw tomatoes.

Walnuts-Omega-3 fatty acids also come from plants. These nuts have the highest concentration around. A good source of protein, fiber and vitamin E, they're also known to lower the risk of heart disease and cholesterol levels. Watch out for the calorie content, though!

Wild Salmon-Our bodies cannot produce omega-3 fatty acids, essential fats we can get from other yummy sources. Salmon, especially wild salmon, is one of the best sources. Omega-3 fatty acids help brain and heart health and there have been recent studies that say it can also protect skin from sun damage and cancer. It's also loaded with Vitamin D.

Yogurt-Any kind, from a goat or cow, is a great source of calcium, protein, B-complex vitamins and it is famous for its good bacteria which keeps harmful ones away as it reduces inflammation and promotes a healthy digestive tract. Here's some good news about yogurt-new research suggests it might help burn fat, especially in the abdominal area.

7 Mood Boosting Foods I Bet You Didn't Know About

"Beware the term 'local delicacy.' It's usually code for something revolting."
Lillian Marsano

Down? Blue-ish? (Really?! You don't look blue-ish!) Did you know that there are intricate connections between certain foods and how we feel, whether it's feeling calmer, more alert or even happy! Many foods that alter your spirit may be already on your kitchen counter. So kick start your day with them to boost your mood:

Bananas
Magnesium deficiency and stress are linked so closely that some doctors and dieticians advise people who lead a hectic life to add magnesium-rich foods like bananas to their diets. Increased magnesium intake results in less anxiety and better sleep. If you don't like bananas, other good magnesium sources are nuts, beans and leafy greens.

Hot Chilies
Capsaicin, the natural ingredient that gives chilies their sting, stimulates the mouth's nerve endings, causing a burning sensation. In response, the brain releases endorphins, natural painkillers that produce a temporary high. So the more hot chilies you eat, the stronger the soothing effect. In fact, some hot-chili lovers may just be hooked on the high.

Oranges and Grapefruits
Even a small deficiency in vitamin C can leave you feeling irritable and blue. A lack of vitamin-C-rich foods also inhibits your body's ability to absorb the iron it needs to fight fatigue. No one wants to eat 6 oranges per day, although this can result in less nervousness, crankiness and depression. I'd suggest a Vitamin C supplement, instead.

Seafood
Seafood contains a lot of selenium, a mineral linked to upbeat moods. (We'll talk about this mineral in a minute.) Increased intake of seafood leads to a greater sense of happiness, more energy and a reduction in anxiety. If you juggle a hectic life, your level of cortisol rises. Stress hormones flood the body during tension and result in lower resistance to cold and viruses and a tired feeling. Be careful if you have high blood pressure, though, as seafood is high in sodium.

Turkey and Chicken
These low-fat protein sources are rich in tyrosine, an amino acid that boosts levels of the brain chemicals dopamine and norepinephrine. These two chemicals are responsible for our motivation and reaction time. Tyrosine lifts energy levels and helps the body cope better with stress. (Can't I just inject a turkey leg into my arm?) Chicken noodle soup may produce the same results. But make sure to sit up straight and don't slurp it!

Whole-Grain Bread

Do your kids drive you batty asking question after question, always being curious? Then you already have a taste of what happens to your brainpower when you eat whole-grain bread. Amino acids are building blocks of proteins and can be found in most foods. One important function of amino acids is to deliver messages to your central nervous system, more commonly known as the brain.

Proteins and amino acids play an important role in normal brain function, particularly before birth when the developing fetus has as much as 3 times as much protein as the mother.

Whole-grain bread is enriched with the essential amino acids as compared to white bread. Now, don't go nuts feeding your family 9 slices each. Just make sure that, when they have a slice of toast, it's not processed. This food helps to increase the transmission speed of nerve impulses in your nervous system.

Water

Mild dehydration is a common but often overlooked cause of fatigue. When the body dehydrates, blood flow to your organs decreases and the body slows down. Drinking enough water each day can prevent you from feeling lethargic. But don't rely on thirst alone. Most adults should drink eight to ten glasses of water per day, depending on their size. Kids should be made aware of the importance of staying hydrated, as well! They should be drinking 5-6 glasses. Caffeinated soft drinks and coffee, however, are no good. They may act as diuretics and increase dehydration. Plus, have you ever seen what happens to cola when it's dripped on the hood of a car?! Frightening!

"No diet will remove all the fat from your body because the brain is entirely fat. Without a brain you might look good, but all you could do is run for public office."

Covert Bailey (fitness expert)

The Best Time of the Year to Buy

The cucumber is *".... about as close to neutrality as a vegetable can get without ceasing to exist."*   **Waverly Root**

Every plant has a growing season, and that's when the fresh produce has the most nutrients and flavor. Stored or frozen foods lose a lot when not in season. Here's a guide to the more common foods and when it's the best time of year to buy them:

Fruits and Vegetables
Apples: October and November
Asparagus: January through March
Avocados: January and February, May and June
Bell peppers: July through October
Blueberries: July and August
Cherries: June
Cucumbers: June Through August
Grapefruit: January through March
Grapes: June through September
Melons: May through August
Navel Oranges: December through February
Peaches and Nectarines: June through September
Pears: November through February (varies with type)
Plums: June through October
Strawberries and Raspberries: grown throughout the US, there is usually a place where they're being harvested all year round. Check with your grocer.
Tomatoes: January through March and July through October

Fish
Alaskan Sockeye Salmon: Mid-May through July
Bluefish: January, April, and December
Cod: January-February and July Through December
Coho Salmon: Mid-August to early October
Halibut: May through early fall
Lake Trout: January and May through November
Mackerel: January through March and May through the end of the year
Red Snapper: Late fall through March
Sea Scallops: Late fall through winter
Sea Trout: August and October through winter
Striped Bass: January and May-June

"We kids feared many things in those days - werewolves, dentists, North Koreans, Sunday school - but they all paled in comparison with Brussels sprouts." **Dave Barry, Miami Herald**

Explanation of Vitamins and Minerals

"Avoid fruits and nuts. You are what you eat."
Jim Davis, 'Garfield'

The following is a list of all the vitamins and minerals that are in the foods included in this book, along with an explanation. I mean, who the heck knows what magnesium does for you? Well, after reading this, you'll know. Won't that make you more fun at parties?

Calcium-Benefits bone health.

Copper-Copper is an essential part of several body enzymes (natural substances required for chemical reactions in the body). It is necessary for iron metabolism, for the formation of the brown pigment *melanin*, in hair and skin, and in the functioning of the body's central nervous system.

Fiber-Protects against coronary heart disease and reduces the risk of diabetes

Folate-Helps produce and maintain new cells. Folate is needed to make DNA and RNA, the building blocks of cells. It also helps prevent changes to DNA that may lead to cancer

Magnesium-Helps maintain muscle and nerve function as well as to help develop and maintain bones. (Enjoy the party…)

Manganese-Manganese is needed for healthy skin, bone, and cartilage formation, as well as glucose tolerance.

Phosphorus-Along with the B vitamins, phosphorus is needed to extract energy from food, particularly fats and starches. It is a component of healthy bones, teeth, gums and many other tissues. Phosphorus also helps with kidney functioning and heart regularity. It lessens arthritis pain. But none of this would be possible without proper levels of vitamin D and calcium, which phosphorus needs to function properly.

Potassium-Helps maintain healthy blood pressure and it helps reduce the effects of salt.

Protein-Protein is the main component of muscles, organs, and glands. Every living cell and all body fluids, except bile and urine, contain protein. The cells of muscles, tendons, and ligaments are maintained with protein. Children and adolescents require protein for growth and development.

Riboflavin-Also known as vitamin B2. Like the other B vitamins, it plays a key role in energy metabolism, and is required for the metabolism of fats, carbohydrates, and proteins.

Selenium-Helps prevent cellular damage from free radicals.

Vitamin A-Important for vision, embryonic development and immune functions.

Vitamin B12-Primary functions are in the formation of red blood cells and the maintenance of a healthy nervous system. B12 is necessary for the rapid synthesis of DNA during cell division

Vitamin C-Acts as a disease-fighting antioxidant

Vitamin E-Also a disease fighting antioxidant

Vitamin K-Vitamin K's primary function is to regulate normal blood clotting

Zinc-It stimulates the activity of approximately 100 enzymes, which are substances that promote biochemical reactions in your body. Zinc supports a healthy immune system, is needed for wound healing, helps maintain your sense of taste and smell and is needed for DNA synthesis. Zinc also supports normal growth and development during pregnancy, childhood, and adolescence.

Breakfast Burritos

Outrageous
Oatmeal

Breakfasts

Ahhh…breakfast. The most important meal of the day. Breaking the overnight fast. It's one of my favorites. (Lunch and Dinner being the others). As a busy, working woman, it's often the only meal where I have true control over what goes into a dish.

Eggs are the "standard" breakfast food. An amazing source of protein, the whites only have about 15 calories each. The yolks have about 55 calories and are full of iron and nutrients, but if you really want to watch your calories for the day, forego these and just use the whites. Use 4 whites and a little butter spray on the pan and you have the basics for thousands of creative breakfast meals. Protein also digests slower, so it keeps you fuller longer without that bloated, stuffed feeling you get with a calorie laden, heavy starch breakfast like pancakes…with sliced bananas…and whipped cream…and real maple syrup. It sounds really good until you eat it. Then what happens? You need a tow truck to move you from the chair to the car, where you fall asleep at the wheel. Who knew pancakes could be so dangerous?

If you DO feel like having something starchy, make sure it's made of whole grains and add a bit of protein, like the terrific oatmeal recipe. This includes vanilla whey protein powder, readily available at better vitamin shops and Whole Foods. I love this recipe on cold days. Living in Southern California, there were 2 in the past 3 years. So, every so often, I eat this standing in front of an open freezer, wearing a ski parka.

If bagels or toast are your thing, or your children's, please make sure they're whole grain. See, this is what happens in your body: When you eat whole grains, it takes a long time for your body to break apart the seed, separate the carbohydrates from the fiber, and completely digest each grain. Your blood sugar rises slowly, stays slightly elevated for a long time (so you don't feel hungry again soon after eating) and never reaches the high levels that come from sugar or refined, white flour. There's no crash, hunger wise, either.

Last note about eating breakfast, then I'll let you read the recipes. If you're not usually a breakfast eater, try to change that, even if it's just a small protein shake or a hard-boiled egg white. Eating starts a process in your body called The Kreb's Cycle. I can get all fancy with long, ridiculous scientific terms, but suffice to say, it jump-starts your metabolism. You'll burn more calories during the day if you eat something when you get up.

And coffee is NOT a breakfast food….

Deviled Crab Egg White Omelet
Prep Time: 20 minutes
Cook Time: 15 minutes
Serves 4

Nutritional Facts:

Calories-142

Total Fat-1g

Sat Fat-0g

Dietary Fiber-1g

Sugars-2g

Sodium- 438 mg

Total Carbohydrates-4g

Trans Fat-0g

Protein-27g

Cholesterol-0g

This dish is very low in saturated fat. It is also a good source of vitamin C, potassium, zinc and copper, and a very good source of protein, vitamin K, riboflavin, vitamin B12 and selenium. Crab is naturally high in sodium, like most shellfish. Live a little.

Ingredients:

Pam butter spray

6 scallions, white and light green part sliced thinly

2 long red chilies, halved lengthwise, seeded and thinly sliced crosswise

2 tsp lemon juice

½ tsp finely grated lemon zest

Pepper

½ lb jumbo lump crabmeat, picked over (can also substitute shrimp)

14 egg whites

1 tbs chopped dill

1 tbs chopped cilantro

In a small skillet, spray Pam butter spray and heat over moderate flame. Add scallions and chilies and cook until softened, about 5 minutes. Add the lemon juice and zest and season with pepper. Transfer to a small bowl. Gently mix in crabmeat. Lightly beat egg whites in separate bowl. Whisk in dill and pepper.

In two 8" non-stick skillets, spray Pam and heat over moderate heat. Pour ½ egg mixture into each skillet. Cook, tilting pan and drawing in the edges of the omelets with a spatula as they set to allow the uncooked white to seep underneath. Flip. Spoon crab mixture over ½ each omelet and fold the omelet over. Slide onto plates, cut in ½ and sprinkle with cilantro.

Fun Food Tip: To see if an egg is fresh, immerse it in a pan of cool, salted water. If it sinks, it's fresh. If it rises to the top, throw it away.

Egg, Mushroom, and Roasted Red-Pepper Burritos
Prep Time: 8 minutes
Cook Time: 20 minutes
Serves 4

Nutritional Facts:

Calories-208

Total Fat-5g

Sat Fat-1g

Dietary Fiber-1g

Sugars-2g

Sodium- 492 mg

Total Carbohydrates-4g

Trans Fat-0g

Protein-12g

Cholesterol-54mg

This food is a good source of vitamin A, and a very good source of vitamin C. Ok, it's a little high in sodium. If you can find a low sodium cheddar cheese that doesn't taste like wet rubber bands, go for it! Then email me the name….

Ingredients:

3 large egg whites

1 large egg

¼ teaspoon pepper

1/2 teaspoon smart balance or Pam butter spray

1 1/2 cups sliced mushrooms

1/2 cup chopped bottled roasted red bell peppers

1/4 cup (1 ounce) low-fat shredded sharp cheddar cheese

4 (8-inch) flour tortillas

1/2 cup bottled salsa

Combine first 3 ingredients in a bowl. Melt butter in a large nonstick skillet over medium heat. Add mushrooms; sauté 10 minutes. Add peppers; sauté 1 minute. Pour egg mixture into pan; cook until bottom begins to set, stirring to scramble. Remove from heat; stir in cheese.

Warm tortillas according to package directions. Spoon one-fourth of egg mixture down center of each tortilla; roll up. Serve with salsa.

Omelet with Summer Vegetables
Prep Time: 30 minutes
Cook Time: 20 minutes
Serves 1

Nutritional Facts:

Calories-275

Total Fat-9g

Sat Fat-4g

Dietary Fiber-2g

Sugars-3g

Sodium- 272 mg

Total Carbohydrates-25g

Trans Fat-0g

Protein-25g

Cholesterol-219

This omelet is a good source of vitamin C, vitamin K, riboflavin and phosphorus and a very good source of protein and selenium. Try making it without the parmesan cheese or substitute soy parmesan cheese. (Honest, it's really good!)

Ingredients:

Cooking spray

1/2 c frozen, low sodium, whole-kernel corn, thawed

1/2 c chopped zucchini

3 tablespoons chopped green onions

2 tablespoons water

¼ tsp black pepper

¼ tsp chili powder

3 large egg whites

1 large egg

2 tablespoons Parmesan cheese.

Heat a small saucepan over medium-high heat. Coat pan with cooking spray. Add corn, zucchini and onions to pan; sauté 4 minutes or until vegetables are crisp-tender. Remove from heat.

Coat a 10-inch nonstick skillet with cooking spray. Heat over medium-high heat. Combine water, pepper, chili powder, egg whites, and egg, stirring well with a whisk. Pour egg mixture into pan; cook until edges begin to set (about 2 minutes). Gently lift the edges of omelet with a spatula, tilting pan to allow uncooked egg mixture to come in contact with pan. Spoon corn mixture onto half of omelet; sprinkle with cheese. Loosen omelet with a spatula, and fold in half over corn mixture. Cook 2 minutes or until the cheese melts. Carefully slide omelet onto a plate.

Asparagus and Leek Frittata
Prep Time: 15 minutes
Cook Time: 15 minutes
Serves 4

Nutritional Facts:

Calories-118

Total Fat-4g

Sat Fat-2g

Dietary Fiber-2g

Sugars-3g

Sodium- 201 mg

Total Carbohydrates-4g

Trans Fat-0g

Protein-12g

Cholesterol-111mg

The frittata is a good source of vitamin A and a very good source of protein, vitamin K, riboflavin and selenium. It is, however, a little high in cholesterol. If you're watching your levels, try this with all egg whites.

Ingredients:

Olive oil spray

1 medium leek, white and some green parts, sliced thin

3/4 pound thin asparagus, sliced into 1" pieces

2 tablespoon fat free, low sodium chicken broth

1/4 teaspoon black pepper

2 tablespoon flat-leaf parsley

1 tablespoon fresh chives

2 egg yolks

8 egg whites

2 tablespoons feta cheese

Preheat the broiler. Spray the oil in a medium nonstick skillet with an ovenproof handle over medium-high heat. Add the leek and cook, stirring often, for 3 minutes, or until soft.

Add the asparagus, broth, 1/8 teaspoon of the pepper, parsley, and chives. Cook, stirring often, for 3 minutes, or until the asparagus is tender-crisp and the broth has evaporated. Spread the asparagus mixture evenly in the bottom of the skillet.

Meanwhile, in a medium bowl, whisk together the eggs, cheese and the remaining 1/8 teaspoon of pepper. Pour into the skillet with the asparagus. Shake the skillet to evenly distribute the egg mixture. Reduce the heat to low, cover, and cook, without stirring, for 3 minutes, or until the eggs begin to set at the edges.

With a spatula, lift up an edge of the frittata and tilt the skillet to allow the uncooked mixture to flow to the bottom of the pan. Place under the broiler. Broil for 1 to 3 minutes, or until the eggs are set on the top and the frittata is lightly puffed.

Cut into wedges to serve.

Herbed Asparagus Omelet

Prep Time: 15 minutes
Cook Time: 25 minutes
Serves 4

Nutritional Facts:

Calories-164
Total Fat-8g
Sat Fat-4g
Dietary Fiber-1g
Sugars-3g

Sodium- 241mg
Total Carbohydrates-4g
Trans Fat-0g
Protein-18g
Cholesterol-218mg

A good source of vitamin A and phosphorus, this omelet is also a very good source of protein, vitamin K, riboflavin and selenium. Again, use all egg whites to lower the cholesterol. As for the sodium, it's the goat cheese. (Try it without it, but it won't be as yummy.)

Ingredients:

Cooking spray
8 egg whites
4 eggs
1/4 cup fat-free milk
2 tablespoons sliced scallions
1/4 cup fresh herbs
1/2 teaspoon ground black pepper
8 ounces asparagus
1/4 cup water
4 tablespoon goat cheese

In a medium bowl, whisk together the egg whites, eggs, and milk. Stir in the scallions, herbs and pepper.

Place the asparagus and water in a large microwave-safe bowl. Cover with vented plastic wrap and microwave on high power for a total of 4 to 6 minutes, or until crisp-tender; stop and stir after 2 minutes. Drain, pat dry, and add to the egg mixture.

Coat a medium nonstick skillet with nonstick spray. Set over medium heat until hot. Pour one-fourth of the egg mixture into the skillet and cook, occasionally scraping the bottom of the skillet, for 2 to 3 minutes. Sprinkle with 1 tablespoon of the goat cheese. Add one-fourth of the asparagus pieces. Continue to cook for 4 to 5 minutes, or until the eggs are almost set.

Using a large spatula, fold the omelet in half. Cook for 3 minutes, or until the omelet is golden and the cheese is melted. Turn onto a plate to keep warm.

Coat the skillet with nonstick spray and repeat the process with the remaining ingredients to make three more omelets.

"If toast always lands butter-side down, and cats always land on their feet, what happens if you strap toast on the back of a cat and drop it?"
Steven Wright

Vegetable Breakfast Quiche
Prep Time: 30 minutes
Cook Time: 1 hour, 20 minutes
Serves 8

Nutritional Facts:

Calories-146

Total Fat-4g

Sat Fat-2g

Dietary Fiber-2g

Sugars-4g

Sodium- 110mg

Total Carbohydrates-17g

Trans Fat-4g

Protein-11g

Cholesterol-63mg

The quiche is a good source of protein, vitamin C, riboflavin, calcium, phosphorus, potassium, manganese and selenium and a very good source of vitamin A and vitamin K. The big question is…will real men eat this?

Ingredients:

1/2 cup water

1/4 cup sun-dried tomatoes

1/2 pound asparagus (about 2 cups chopped) or broccoli florets

1/2 medium onion, chopped

2 cloves garlic, sliced

2 tablespoons olive oil

1 carrot cut in small cubes (about 1 cup)

5 mushrooms, sliced

1 tablespoon chopped fresh basil, or 1 teaspoon dried

1 tablespoon chopped fresh parsley

1/8 teaspoon chili flakes

1/8 teaspoon freshly grated nutmeg

1 teaspoon freshly ground black pepper

3 small red potatoes, washed and thinly sliced

1/2 cup grated cheese, low fat pepper jack or swiss

1/4 cup fat free milk

1/2 cup low-fat sour cream

2 eggs

5 egg whites

1 medium tomato, sliced (seeds squeezed out)

3 tablespoons soy Parmesan cheese

Boil the water, pour over the sun-dried tomatoes, and allow to soak for about 15 minutes until they become soft and plump. Strain off any remaining liquid, and coarsely chop.

Cut off about 1 inch of the coarse ends of the asparagus stalks and discard or save them for soup. Cut the remaining stalks into about 6 pieces or chop coarsely. If you are using broccoli, cut into florets. Blanch the asparagus by boiling it in a medium pot of water for 2 minutes or less. Asparagus should be bright green and firm to the bite.

Drain, rinse the asparagus in cold water, and drain again in a colander.

Sauté the onions and the garlic in the olive oil over low heat until the onions are transparent, approximately 10 minutes. Add the carrots, mushrooms, basil, parsley, chili flakes, nutmeg, and pepper and continue to cook for 5 minutes more. Remove from the heat.

Lightly grease the bottom and sides of a 9-inch pie pan. Line the bottom with the potato slices, overlapping them slightly. Whisk together the cheese, milk, sun-dried tomatoes, sour cream, and the eggs in a large bowl. Mix in the sautéed vegetables and the blanched asparagus, coating everything with the cheese, milk, and egg liquid, then pour into the potato-lined pie pan. Arrange the tomato slices on top and sprinkle with Parmesan cheese. Bake for 1 hour, covering after 45 minutes if top browns. Completely baked quiche should be very firm. Let cool 15 minutes before slicing and serving. Leftovers can be wrapped and kept in the refrigerator for up to 3 days.

Fun Food Tip: To prevent eggshells from cracking, add a pinch of salt to the water before hard-boiling.

Power Muffins
Prep Time: 10 minutes
Cook Time: 35 minutes
12 Muffins

Nutritional Facts:

Calories-163

Total Fat-3g

Sat Fat-2g

Dietary Fiber-6g

Sugars-4g

Sodium- 77mg

Total Carbohydrates-30g

Trans Fat-0g

Protein-9g

Cholesterol-63mg

This muffin recipe comes from my friend, Beth (my first roomie after college!) who actually went into business selling these. They've got a lot goin' on and the taste explodes in your mouth. Try them with the optional ingredients! These muffins will keep you full for hours! They're high in potassium, calcium and vitamin A.

Ingredients:
1 cup unprocessed wheat bran
1 cup oat bran
12 oz fat-free, sugar-free yogurt
1-1/3 cups dry nonfat milk
1 cup unsweetened applesauce
10 tbsp raisins
6 tbsp soy flour
2 tsp each: baking powder, baking soda
2 tbsp cinnamon
6 pkgs stevia
2 tbsp vanilla

OPTIONAL INGREDIENTS:
1/3 cup ground flax seed
1/3 cup wheat germ
½ cup walnuts

Pre-heat oven to 350. Spray 2 6-muffin tins with cooking spray. Mix all ingredients together. Spoon batter evenly into tins. Bake 350 degrees until toothpick comes out clean. (First try should be about 40-45 minutes)

This is a great recipe to be creative with. Try using bananas, dried cranberries and almonds or dried blueberries and mangoes! Thanks, Bethsky!

"There is a vast difference between the savage and the civilized man, but it is never apparent to their wives until after breakfast."

Helen Rowland (1876-1950) *A Guide to Men*

Outrageous Oatmeal
Prep Time: 5 minutes
Cook Time: 3 minutes
Serves 1

Nutritional Facts:

Calories-370

Total Fat-6g

Sat Fat-1g

Dietary Fiber-11g

Sugars-8g

Sodium- 96mg

Total Carbohydrates-57g

Trans Fat-0g

Protein-18g

Cholesterol-30mg

This is my favorite carbohydrate breakfast. It's a great meal for kids and adults who want a hot breakfast that will keep them full ALL morning. When I eat this, I can go for at least 4 hours without needing a mid-morning snack. That's because of the high protein content. The sugar is from the blueberries, which are low on the glycemic index and have a ton of antioxidants. Also, if you're going to have starchy carbohydrates, eat them in the morning so they'll be digested and the energy from them used during the day. Eat this, then you'll have lots of energy for a 3 or 4 mile run.

Like you have time for that.

Ingredients:

¾ c plain quick cooking oatmeal (I like McCann's)

1 cup water, more or less

½ c blueberries

A sprinkle of cinnamon

½ scoop (22 g) vanilla or banana flavored protein powder

OPTIONAL INGREDIENTS:

2 Tbs toasted almond slivers

Place the oatmeal in a microwaveable bowl. Pour the water over it, just enough so that the oatmeal absorbs most of it. Place in the microwave for 2 minutes. When done, stir. If a looser consistency is preferred, add a touch more water, stir and microwave for another 30 seconds. Mix in all other ingredients. I like the optional almonds as it adds a nice crunch. While they add about 150 calories and 15 grams of fat, your body needs this healthy fat. Plus, they have vitamin E and manganese.

Fun Food Tip: Oatmeal isn't just for breakfast anymore! It can soothe arthritis pain. Mix 2 cups of regular oatmeal and one cup of water in a bowl. Warm it in the microwave for one minute. Cool slightly and apply the mix to your hands or wherever you have discomfort.

Cherry Tomatoes
with Watermelon

Watercress and
Orange Salad

Salads

I have a theory as to how salads were invented. It goes all the way back to the cavemen...the original hunter-gatherers. While the men were out hunting Wooly Mammoths for the weekly neighborhood bar-b-q, the women were out gathering everything else. As they foraged through the forests and fields, picking dandelion leaves, fruits and nuts, did they have sacks with sections? I don't think so! So what happened? They threw everything...greens, nuts, berries, all into one big animal-skin bag. By the time they got back to their big fire pit/cook area, everything was all jumbled together in the bag. They spilled out the contents and what did they have? Tossed salad!!!

But...that's just my theory.

Today's salad fixin' possibilities are endless. As seen here, you can be very creative with ingredients and seasonings. Use these recipes as a base as well as on their own. Add steak to the cherry tomato and watermelon salad. Throw some grilled tofu in with the eggplant salad, or use your leftover veggies from dinner last night to give your salad a little more pizzazz. There'll be no stopping you! It's a great way to practice your cooking creativity ('cause if someone doesn't like what you put in, it's easy to pick it out).

Have fun!

Watercress and Orange Salad

Prep Time: 10 minutes
Cook Time: 15 minutes
Serves 4

Nutritional Facts:

Calories-173
Total Fat-14g
Sat Fat-2g
Dietary Fiber-5g
Sugars-5g

Sodium- 66mg
Total Carbohydrates-11g
Trans Fat-0g
Protein-3g
Cholesterol-0mg

This refreshing salad is low in sodium, and very low in cholesterol. It is also a good source of dietary fiber and manganese, and a very good source of vitamin A, vitamin C, vitamin K and folate. This is one of my favorite "Mom" salads.

Ingredients:

2 bunches watercress
1 head of endive
1 orange, peeled and sectioned
1 small red onion, chopped

Dressing:

2 tsp dijon mustard
¼ tsp ground cumin
3 TBSP red wine vinegar
¼ cup olive oil
Pepper

Clean and tear watercress into bite- sized pieces. Clean and separate Endive leaves. Mix two together in large salad bowl. Sprinkle red onion and arrange orange on top. Whisk all dressing ingredients in small bowl and serve on the side.

Tomato and Zucchini Salad
Prep Time: 20 minutes
Cook Time: 10 minutes
Serves 4

Nutritional Facts:

Calories-155
Total Fat-14g
Sat Fat-2g
Dietary Fiber-2g
Sugars-4g

Sodium- 17mg
Total Carbohydrates-7g
Trans Fat-0g
Protein-2g
Cholesterol-0mg

This salad is very low in cholesterol and sodium. It is also a good source of vitamin A, vitamin B6 and manganese, and a very good source of vitamin C and vitamin K.

Ingredients:
4 small zucchini, about ¾ pound
2 red, ripe tomatoes, about 1-½ pounds
Fresh pepper
1 ½ tsp finely minced garlic
1 TBS finely chopped fresh basil
1 TBS finely chopped fresh parsley
2 TBS red wine vinegar
¼ cup extra virgin olive oil

Trim off ends of the zucchini. Cut each crosswise into thirds. Cut each third lengthwise into quarters. Drop zucchini into a saucepan with boiling water to cover. Add pinch of salt to water. Bring to a boil and simmer 2 minutes. Drain well. Core tomatoes and cut into ½" slices. Arrange slices on a plate. Sprinkle with pepper. Scatter zucchini over the tomatoes. Blend garlic, basil, parsley and sprinkle over veggies. Sprinkle with vinegar and olive oil. Serve.

"Only in dreams are carrots as big as bears."
Yiddish Saying (OK, What the heck does THIS mean?!)

Tomato and Sweet Pepper Salad
Prep Time: 40 minutes
Cook Time: 10 minutes
Serves 4

Nutritional Facts:

Calories-132

Total Fat-8g

Sat Fat-1g

Dietary Fiber-5g

Sugars-10g

Sodium- 16mg

Total Carbohydrates-16g

Trans Fat-0g

Protein-3g

Cholesterol-0mg

This salad is very low in cholesterol and sodium. It is also a good source of dietary fiber, vitamin E, folate, potassium and manganese, and a very good source of vitamin A, vitamin C, vitamin K and vitamin B6. It's terrific for a barbeque!

Ingredients:

6 ripe tomatoes, peeled, seeded and chopped

3 red peppers, roasted, peeled, seeded and diced (can use jarred to save time)

2 Tbs fresh lemon juice

1 tsp fresh ground pepper

2 Tbs extra virgin olive oil

2 Tbs chopped fresh flat leaf parsley

1 small hot chili pepper, seeded and finely minced

½ tsp ground cumin

1 clove garlic, finely minced

Place the tomatoes, red peppers, lemon juice, pepper and oil in a salad bowl. Toss. Add chili pepper, cumin and garlic. Toss again and serve at room temperature.

Moroccan Carrot Salad
Prep Time: 20 minutes
Cook Time: 10 minutes
Serves 4

Nutritional Facts:

Calories-86

Total Fat-4g

Sat Fat-1g

Dietary Fiber-2g

Sugars-6g

Sodium- 82mg

Total Carbohydrates-13g

Trans Fat-0g

Protein-2g

Cholesterol-0mg

I thought I'd throw in a few ethnic dishes here and there. This one is from my buddy Nissim. This is a great side dish for lamb or beef. Actually, I hate cooked carrots, but these are really parboiled, so they still have a little crunch to them. You could even make it with raw carrots. If you do, I'd suggest mincing them. This is a good source of dietary fiber, vitamin B6, potassium and manganese, and a very good source of vitamin A, vitamin C and vitamin K.

Ingredients:

2 lbs of fresh carrots

4-5 garlic pieces minced

1/2 bunch parsley, chopped well

Olive oil to taste

2-2 1/2 squeezed lemons

Cumin powder to taste

Cayenne pepper to taste

Parboil the carrots in water until just soft, only so much that you can easily cut them. Drain the water and cut carrots with a sharp paring knife into 1/4-/1/2 inch rings. You can also make matchstick pieces. Put them back into the pot you cooked in (without any water), add parsley, garlic, olive oil, lemon, cayenne and cumin powder. Mix well, but be careful not to mush the carrots. Let it cool, then put in fridge for an hour.

"I never drink water. I'm afraid it will become habit-forming."
W.C. Fields (1880-1946)

Heirloom Tomato, Lime and Onion Salad
Prep Time: 18 minutes
Cook Time: 1 hour, 5 minutes
Serves 4

Nutritional Facts:

Calories-59

Total Fat-0g

Sat Fat-0g

Dietary Fiber-3g

Sugars-6g

Sodium- 8mg

Total Carbohydrates-14g

Trans Fat-0g

Protein-2g

Cholesterol-0mg

This combo salad is very low in saturated fat, cholesterol and sodium. It is also a good source of dietary fiber, vitamin A, vitamin K, vitamin B6, folate, potassium and manganese, and a very good source of vitamin C. I love heirloom tomatos and their smooth sweetness is a perfect complement to the spicy onion and tart lime.

Ingredients:

4 cups sliced red onion

¼ c fresh limejuice

1 cup chopped heirloom tomatoes

¼ c chopped fresh cilantro

Pepper to taste

½ tsp grated lime rind

Combine first 3 ingredients in medium bowl. Let stand at room temperature for about an hour. Stir in rest of ingredients. Serve.

Fun Food Tip: Cure a headache with lime! Cut a lime in half and rub it on your forehead. The throbbing will go away.

Grilled Eggplant Salad
Prep time: 15 minutes
Cook Time: 15 minutes
Serves 4

Nutritional Facts:
Calories-132

Total Fat-8g

Sat Fat-1g

Dietary Fiber-5g

Sugars-10g

Sodium- 16mg

Total Carbohydrates-16g

Trans Fat-0g

Protein-3g

Cholesterol-0mg

Don't overdo the olive oil in this recipe as eggplant absorbs it quickly. That being said, this is very low in cholesterol and sodium. It is also a good source of dietary fiber and manganese, and a very good source of vitamin K.

Ingredients:
2 cloves of garlic, minced
¼ cup olive oil
2 eggplants peeled and cut lengthwise into slices about ½" thick
Fresh ground pepper
¼ cup red wine vinegar
Chopped mint or flat leaf parsley

Pre-heat the grill. In a small bowl stir the garlic into the oil and brush the eggplant slices on both sides with the oil. Sprinkle both sides with pepper and place on a grill rack. Turn once, after about 2minutes and cook until tender. Transfer to a serving platter and sprinkle with the vinegar and mint or parsley. Let cool for 15 minutes.

Asian Slaw
Prep Time: 20 minutes
Cook Time: 15 minutes
Serves 4

Nutritional Facts:

Calories-89

Total Fat-3g

Sat Fat-0g

Dietary Fiber-6g

Sugars-6g

Sodium-39mg

Total Carbohydrates-16g

Trans Fat-0g

Protein-3g

Cholesterol-0mg

I have never been a big fan of regular cole slaw, but this one is special, with a nice kick from spicy chilies! It's low in sodium, and very low in cholesterol. It is also a good source of thiamin and potassium, and a very good source of dietary fiber, vitamin A, vitamin C, vitamin K, vitamin B6, folate and manganese.

Ingredients:

5 tablespoon seasoned rice vinegar

4 tablespoon fresh lime juice

1 packet stevia

2 teaspoons grapeseed or canola oil

2 teaspoons finely grated, peeled fresh gingerroot

1 to 2 teaspoons finely chopped, seeded hot red chili,

8 cup thinly sliced Napa cabbage (about 1 pound)

2 carrots, thinly sliced

1 red bell pepper, thinly sliced

3 scallions, cut into small pieces

½ c coarsely chopped fresh mint leaves

In a large salad bowl, whisk together vinegar, limejuice, stevia, oil, ginger and red chile. Add remaining ingredients.

Toss and let stand, uncovered, at room temperature, 15 minutes before serving.

Cherry Tomatoes with Watermelon
Prep Time: 15 minutes
Cook Time: 8 minutes
Serves 4

Nutritional Facts:

Calories-216

Total Fat-5g

Sat Fat-0g

Dietary Fiber-3g

Sugars-35g

Sodium- 13mg

Total Carbohydrates-46g

Trans Fat-0g

Protein-4g

Cholesterol-0mg

This salad is actually a fruit salad…tomatoes really being a fruit and all. That's why it's a little high in sugar, but the good part is that it's low in saturated fat, and very low in cholesterol and sodium. It is also a very good source of vitamin A and vitamin C.

Ingredients:

1/2 pint yellow cherry or grape tomatoes

1/2 pint red cherry or grape tomatoes

1 small seedless watermelon (red or yellow)

1/2 teaspoon coriander seeds

1/4 teaspoon white or red peppercorns

1 tablespoon extra-virgin olive oil

1 tablespoon slivered fresh mint leaves

Slice half the yellow and half the red tomatoes in halves and place in a large bowl along with the remaining whole tomatoes. Slice the melon into similar size cubes (or use a melon baller) and add to bowl. (You should have about 4 cups of melon.)

Crush the coriander and peppercorns in a mortar and pestle until coarsely ground (or, alternatively, place in a clean linen kitchen towel and pound with a mallet). Sprinkle on tomatoes and melon. Add olive oil and mint and gently toss to coat.

Fun Food Tip: Wrap celery in aluminum foil when putting it in the refrigerator. It will keep for weeks!

Tofu Salad
Prep Time: 30 minutes
Cook Time: 15 minutes
Serves 4

Nutritional Facts:
Calories-175

Total Fat-6g

Sat Fat-1g

Dietary Fiber-2g

Sugars-7g

Sodium- 391 mg

Total Carbohydrates-17g

Trans Fat-0g

Protein-15g

Cholesterol-0mg

My friend, Susan, is a vegan. She loves what I do, but tells me I don't have enough recipes for people like her. So, this is one she gave me, with a little re-engineering on my part. I hope you like it! This food is very low in cholesterol. It is also a good source of phosphorus and copper, and a very good source of protein, vitamin A and vitamin C.

Ingredients:
2 14 oz. containers of firm tofu. Drain and squeeze by hand into a coarse paste.
2 heaping tbsp. umeboshi paste (Japanese plum paste found in health food stores. It's pretty easy to find…I promise!)
2 tbsp. red wine vinegar
2 tbsp. toasted sesame oil
2 tbsp. tamari (low sodium)
1/2 cup finely diced carrot
1/2 cup finely diced bell pepper
1/2 cup corn cut fresh from the cob
1/2 cup finely chopped red onion
1/2 cup finely chopped cilantro (or any other green herb such as basil)

Make a marinade by mixing together the umeboshi paste, red wine vinegar, toasted sesame oil, and tamari in a small bowl. Blanche the carrot, bell pepper, and corn in boiling water for 3 minutes, rinse in cold water until cool, and drain thoroughly. Combine all with the red onion and cilantro in a large bowl. Add the marinade, stir, and allow it to sit for 5 minutes. Add the mashed tofu and mix well. Chill for at least 2 hours. As much water as possible must be squeezed out of the tofu and the blanched vegetables.

The tofu salad may be scooped with an ice cream scoop and served on a bed of greens. It can also be served as a dip with chips or as a sandwich filling in pita bread with lettuce and sliced tomatoes. Other vegetable combinations may be used, and if necessary, frozen vegetables may be substituted for fresh. The recipe makes about 5 cups and is best if consumed within two days. To make a smaller amount, use only one container of tofu and cut the other ingredients in half.

Spicy Red
Pepper Soup

Cold Cream of Cucumber Soup

<u>*Soups*</u>

"First prepare the soup of your choice and pour it into a bowl. Then, take the bowl and quickly turn it upside down on the cookie tray. Lift the bowl ever so gently so that the soup retains the shape of the bowl. Gently is the key word here. Then, with the knife cut the soup down the middle into halves, then quarters, and gently reassemble the soup into a cube. Some of the soup will run off onto the cookie tray. Lift this soup up by the corners and fold slowly into a cylindrical soup staff. Place the packet in your purse or inside coat pocket, and pack off to work."
Steve Martin

Soup is the ultimate comfort food for me. It's a fun way to have a one-dish meal, too! I prefer "busy" soups…soups with lots of stuff in 'em; lots of flavors melding together, textures to chew on, etc. I can appreciate the simple pleasure of hot, plain chicken stock when one is sick, but I usually consider plain stock a blank canvas—with an unending array of interesting possible ingredients with which to experiment.

When I was a kid, my Mom made what was affectionately known as "Garbage Soup." Why? Because she put all kind of "garbage" in it. It has a beef broth base and she threw in all kinds of greens, short ribs, soup bones, barley, root vegetables, beans, you name it. I think one time there was even a dive mask and snorkel in it. She must have lost it while stirring. The thing is, it never came out exactly the same way twice. Could have been creativeness, could have been that she was too lazy to measure. There was no telling.

This was the ultimate one-dish meal with protein, starch and vegetables. Of course, it wasn't by "weight management" standards as "low carb/ low fat/ low salt" as I'd like, but heck, I was twelve! And it was great.

My point is that there is no specific formula for the comfort of soup. It can be thick and hearty or plain and light. (Or in my best friend, Weeny's case—comfort is peanut butter and bacon on whole-wheat toast, but that's not even a soup and frankly…I have no idea how to re-engineer this one, anyway.)

Mom's Garbage Soup recipe is included here and I did the best I could to re-engineer it and still do it justice. It brought back a lot of memories. Especially when I pretended I was twelve, whined a lot and complained that my brothers were picking on me.

Wait. I do that now.

Wild Mushroom Stock
Prep Time: 25 minutes
Cook Time: 1 hour, 10 minutes
Serves 4

Nutritional Facts:

Calories-45

Total Fat-0g

Sat Fat-0g

Dietary Fiber-2g

Sugars-3g

Sodium- 33mg

Total Carbohydrates-10g

Trans Fat-0g

Protein-2g

Cholesterol-0mg

I love this stock. It's very low in saturated fat and cholesterol. It is also a good source of dietary fiber, vitamin C, vitamin B6, folate, phosphorus and selenium, and a very good source of vitamin A, vitamin K, riboflavin, niacin, pantothenic acid, potassium, copper and manganese. Use it instead of chicken broth for an earthier flavor!

Ingredients:

1 oz dried porcini mushrooms

Olive oil spray

4 oz fresh crimini or Portobello mushrooms, sliced or chopped

2 medium carrots, peeled and diced

2 celery stalks, diced

1 medium onion, chopped small

1 leek, roughly chopped

½ tsp dried thyme

¼ cup fresh parsley, chopped

2 bay leaves

½ tsp dried sage

3 garlic cloves, chopped

9 cups of cold water

1 cup hot water

Cover the dried mushrooms with the hot water and set aside. Spray 8 qt. soup pot with olive oil spray. Over med-high heat, add all the vegetables, herbs, garlic and cook for about 5 minutes. Add the dried mushrooms and soaking liquid, as well as all the cold water.   Bring to a boil and simmer for 45 minutes. Strain through a fine-mesh sieve. Use as a base for other dishes, or alone, if you're a purist. Makes 6 to 8 cups.

Tomato Soup with Roasted Red Peppers
Prep Time: 20 minutes
Cook Time: 1 hour, 10 minutes
Serves 4

Nutritional Facts:

Calories-56
Total Fat-1g
Sat Fat-0g
Dietary Fiber-2g
Sugars-5g

Sodium- 37mg
Total Carbohydrates-10g
Trans Fat-0g
Protein-4g
Cholesterol-0mg

Tomato soup is one of my most favorite winter foods. (Is hot cocoa considered food?) Anyway, I like this recipe because it's got the sweet zing of red pepper. It's low in saturated fat, and very low in cholesterol. It is also a good source of dietary fiber, niacin, folate, phosphorus, potassium, copper and manganese, and a very good source of vitamin A, vitamin C, vitamin K and vitamin B6.

Ingredients:
Olive oil spray
1 1/2 lbs red bell peppers, halved and seeded
3 medium, ripe plum tomatoes, halved
2 onions, unpeeled and quartered
5 garlic cloves, unpeeled
2 ½ cups low sodium chicken stock
Pepper to taste
2 Tbs fresh basil, torn

Optional:
Soy Parmesan cheese as garnish

Preheat oven to 400 degrees. Spray large roasting pan and place the bell peppers and tomatoes cut side down in the pan with the onions and the garlic. Spray veggies again. Cook in the oven for 30 minutes or until skins on the bell peppers have started to blacken and blister. Let the veggies cool for about 10 minutes, and then remove skins, stalks and seeds from bell peppers. Peel away skins from the tomatoes and onions and squeeze out the garlic. Place all ingredients except basil and stock in a blender or food processor and blend until smooth. Add stock and blend again to form a puree. Pour back into a saucepan and bring to a boil. Lower heat and simmer for 2-3 minutes and season with pepper. Serve hot, sprinkled with basil.

Sweet Pepper Soup
Prep Time: 15 minutes
Cook Time: 25 minutes
Serves 4

Nutritional Facts:

Calories-176

Total Fat-8g

Sat Fat-4g

Dietary Fiber-6g

Sugars-13g

Sodium- 53g

Total Carbohydrates-26g

Trans Fat-0g

Protein-5g

Cholesterol-20g

This is a nice soup if you like a creamy consistancy. Try fat free greek-style yogurt in this. It tastes exactly like sour cream! The health benefits of this soup are as follows: it is low in saturated fat, and very low in cholesterol. It is also a good source of dietary fiber, protein, vitamin E,vitamin K, riboflavin, niacin, calcium, phosphorus, potassium and manganese, and a very good source of vitamin A, vitamin C, vitamin B6 and folate.

Ingredients:

2 cups chopped onions

Olive oil spray

6 cups chopped red, yellow and orange peppers (about 2 of each)

2 cups low sodium vegetable stock

1 cup low fat sour cream or plain, fat free yogurt

1/3 cup chopped fresh dill

2 TBS lemon juice

Ground pepper to taste

In a soup pot, spray olive oil to cover the bottom. Over medium heat, sauté the onions until just soft, about 3 minutes. Add bell peppers and cook, covered, until just soft, stirring occasionally. In a blender or food processor, whirl the cooked veggies with the stock, low fat sour cream, dill and lemon juice. Consistency should be just under pureed. Return soup to pot, reheat, and add ground pepper to taste.

Spicy Red Pepper Soup
Prep Time: 40 minutes
Cook Time: About 2 hours with cool-down time
Serves 4

Nutritional Facts:

Calories-113

Total Fat-3g

Sat Fat-0g

Dietary Fiber-6g

Sugars-8g

Sodium- 33mg

Total Carbohydrates-22g

Trans Fat-0g

Protein-4g

Cholesterol-0mg

This soup has a nice kick to it. You can add fat free sour cream, or my favorite, Trader Joe's non-fat reek-style yogurt. It's full of fiber, low in calories and has vitamin A, vitamin C, vitamin K, vitamin B6 and folate.

Ingredients:

1 or 2 ancho chilies

Olive oil spray

¼ tsp marjoram

¼ tsp thyme

¼ tsp sage

2 bay leaves

2 cloves

5 cloves of garlic, chopped

1 medium red onion, sliced

1 leek, white part only, sliced

1 lb red peppers, seeded and sliced

1 lb ripe roma tomatoes, peeled, seeded and chopped, juice reserved

6 cups water

8 oz small green cabbage, chopped

Chopped parsley for garnish

Remove the stems, seeds and veins from the chilies. Tear the flesh into a few large pieces. Cover them with water, bring to a boil and simmer 20 minutes. Puree in a blender.

Spray a soup pot with the olive oil spray. Over low heat, warm the pot and add the mixed herbs, bay leaves and cloves until fragrant. Add garlic and cook about 30 seconds. Stir in onion, leek and peppers. Stir well to coat vegetables with any oil. Cover the pot and leave on low heat. Check after 5 minutes and stir. If veggies stick, add ½ cup water. After another 5-10 minutes, add tomatoes, 4 tablespoons of chili puree and 6 cups of water. Bring to a boil and lower to simmer. Add cabbage, cover with lid and cook slowly for 40 minutes. Let soup cool for about ½ hour, then puree for 1 minute. Return to pot. Stir and ladle into bowls. Garnish with parsley. Serves 4-6.

Spicy Kale Chowder with Turkey or Chicken Sausage
Prep Time: 40 minutes
Cook Time: 45 minutes
Serves 10

Nutritional Facts:

Calories-176

Total Fat-7g

Sat Fat-2g

Dietary Fiber-1g

Sugars-6g

Sodium- 577 mg

Total Carbohydrates-15g

Trans Fat-0g

Protein-14g

Cholesterol-35mg

Many sausages are high in sodium, hence the breakdown here. If you can find one that's lower in sodium, try it and let me know how it is! Many canned plum tomatoes now come in a low sodium version, also. This has a good amount of protein and kale isn't bitter at all when cooked with the tomatoes. The ginger is a nice twist. You can also leave it out and substitute a ½ jalapeno pepper for some REAL spice.

Ingredients:

Pam cooking spray

8 garlic cloves, thinly sliced

2 large onions, finely chopped

2 tbs minced fresh ginger

1 pound low fat spicy turkey or chicken sausage. Slice ¼' thick

1 28 oz can Italian Plum tomatoes, chopped, with juices reserved

3 quarts low sodium turkey or chicken broth

¾ lb kale, large stems and ribs discarded, leaves coarsely chopped. About 8 cups worth.

Pepper to taste

Spray Pam in bottom of large soup pot. Add garlic and onions and cook over moderate heat, stirring occasionally until softened. About 12 minutes. Add ginger and sausage and cook for 5 minutes, stirring occasionally. Add the tomatoes and juices. Bring to a boil. Add the stock and kale and return to a boil.

Reduce heat to moderate and simmer the soup until kale is tender, about 10 minutes. Season with pepper and serve. Make ahead and freeze, as well.

"I'm at the age where food has taken the place of sex in my life.
In fact, I've just had a mirror put over my kitchen table."

Rodney Dangerfield

Southwest Shrimp Soup
Prep Time: 20 min
Cook Time: 15 min
Serves 4

Nutritional Facts:

Calories-279

Total Fat-5g

Sat Fat-1g

Dietary Fiber-7g

Sugars-1g

Sodium- 564 mg

Total Carbohydrates-30g

Trans Fat-0g

Protein-29g

Cholesterol-164mg

This is a hearty, flavorful soup that's easy and filling. Add some low carb tortillas and a salad and you've got dinner! It's high in protein, fiber and selenium, but watch the sodium if you've got high blood pressure.

Ingredients:

½ cup fat free sour cream

1 tsp ground cumin

1 tsp ground chili powder

Pam cooking spray

3 thinly sliced garlic cloves

4 roma tomatoes, chunked or 1 15 oz can diced, undrained

½ tsp black pepper

2 jalapeno peppers, seeded and thinly sliced

1 15 oz can pinto beans

1 lb raw medium shrimp, peeled and deveined

½ cup fresh cilantro leaves

1 lime, quartered

In a small bowl, mix sour cream, cumin and chili powder. Cover and refrigerate. Spray oil on large saucepan over med-high heat. Add garlic and cook for about a minute. Add the tomatoes with juice, pepper and bring to a simmer. Cook for 10 minutes. Add the jalapenos and pinto beans. Simmer for 5 minutes. Add shrimp and simmer until cooked through, about 3-5 minutes. Ladle the soup into the bowls and top with a spoonful of the sour cream mix. Add the cilantro. Serve lime on the side.

Onion Soup
Prep Time: 10 minutes
Cook Time: 1 hour
Serves 4

__Nutritional Facts:__

Calories-85

Total Fat-2g

Sat Fat-0g

Dietary Fiber-3g

Sugars-7g

Sodium- 320 mg

Total Carbohydrates-15g

Trans Fat-0g

Protein-2g

Cholesterol-0mg

I remember ordering onion soup when it was cold out and getting this wonderful crock topped with cheese. Well, this recipe doesn't have that. C'mon. Do you know how many calories were in that one piece of gooey, yummy, crusty goodness? Let's just say lots, along with about 18 grams of fat. This way is much better. See how low in calories it is? And you can control any extras you want to add to it. So, if you need to add cheese, make it low fat, please. You don't want to clog your arteries or anything. That would be bad. By the way, onions contain the antioxidant quercetin, which helps protect cells from free-radical damage.

Ingredients:
Butter spray

4 large yellow onions, thinly sliced

½ tsp dry mustard

Dash of thyme

4 cups of water

2 tbs low sodium soy sauce

3 tbs dry white wine

Pepper to taste

Spray bottom of soup pot with butter spray. Add onions and cook over medium-low heat for about 10-13 minutes, stirring occasionally. Add mustard and thyme. Stir and cover. Continue cooking over low heat, about 30 minutes more, checking occasionally. If onions start to stick, add ¼ cup vegetable stock. The onions will be very soft and simmering in their own liquid. Add water, soy sauce, wine and pepper. Simmer about 10 minutes more. Serve.

Minestrone
Prep Time: 30 minutes
Cook Time: 45-55 minutes
Serves 6

Nutritional Facts:

Calories-145

Total Fat-3g

Sat Fat-0g

Dietary Fiber-7g

Sugars-9g

Sodium- 59 mg

Total Carbohydrates-27g

Trans Fat-0g

Protein-7g

Cholesterol-0mg

Minestrone is a storehouse of nutritional excellence! Tons of vitamin A, vitamin C, iron, vitamin K, potassium…I could keep going. Lots of fiber and vitamin C, too. Make a lot of this and freeze the extra. There's a lot to chop, so this way you can defrost it when you need it!

Ingredients:
Pam olive oil spray
4-5 cloves of garlic
1 cup chopped onion
½ chopped carrots
1 cup chopped celery
1 cup chopped broccoli
1 cup chopped spinach
½ tsp black pepper
¼ cup fresh basil
1 cup chopped red pepper
1 tsp dried oregano
3 ½ c water
2 c low sodium tomato puree
1 ½ c chick peas

Optional:
½ cup dry pasta
½ cup grated Soy Parmesan cheese

Spray Pam in heavy bottom 4 qt. pot. Add garlic and onion and sauté until soft and translucent. Stir in carrots, celery, broccoli and spinach. Add oregano, pepper and basil. Cover and cook over low heat for 5-8 minutes. Add red pepper, water, tomato puree and beans. Cover and simmer for 15 minutes. Add tomatoes and simmer 10 more minutes. Serve with soy cheese on the side.

Optional: Add pasta and simmer for about 10 more minutes until pasta is al dente.

Lentil Spinach Soup
Prep Time: 25 minutes
Cook Time: 45 minutes
Serves 4

Nutritional Facts:

Calories-238
Total Fat-3g
Sat Fat-0g
Dietary Fiber-19g
Sugars-2g

Sodium- 115 mg
Total Carbohydrates-39g
Trans Fat-0g
Protein-17g
Cholesterol-0mg

A great choice for vegans, this soup is hearty, is high in protein and fiber and very satisfying. I prefer brown lentils for this one, but use either. Balsamic vinegar makes it a little mellower than the red wine vinegar, should you like to try it.

Ingredients:

1 cup green or brown lentils, cleaned and rinsed
1 bay leaf
1 celery stalk, diced
7 cups cold water
Olive oil spray
1 medium onion, chopped
3 garlic cloves, minced
3 tbs fresh parsley
3 medium tomatoes, fresh, peeled, seeded and chopped, reserving juice.
1 lb of cleaned spinach
Red wine vinegar to taste
Pepper

Optional:

Soy Parmesan

Put the lentils, bay leaf and celery in a soup pot with the water and reserved juice from the tomatoes. Bring to a boil and scoop off any foam. Lower heat to slow boil. While the lentils are cooking, spray olive oil into a large skillet and add the onion. Cook for a few minutes and lower the heat. Stir in garlic and parsley. Cook until onion is soft. Add tomatoes and cook for 5 minutes. Combine with lentils. Cut spinach into ½" strips. When lentils are soft, stir in spinach by handfuls. Once it has cooked down, thin the soup, if necessary, with a bit more water. Simmer another 5 minutes and add the vinegar, to taste. Serve with fresh ground pepper and soy cheese.

Hot and Sour Soup
Prep Time: 45 minutes
Cook Time: 40 minutes
Serves 4

Nutritional Facts:

Calories-130

Total Fat-3g

Sat Fat-1g

Dietary Fiber-1g

Sugars-2g

Sodium- 383 mg

Total Carbohydrates-12g

Trans Fat-0g

Protein-12g

Cholesterol-0mg

I've always loved Hot and Sour Soup. It was my "test" dish when I went out to Chinese restaurants. If the soup wasn't good, I knew the rest of the meal wouldn't be, either. Now, I have no excuse! While a little high in sodium, this dish is a good source of riboflavin, pantothenic acid and phosphorus, and a very good source of protein and copper.

Ingredients:
1 oz dried Chinese black mushrooms
8 cups water
3 tbs Chinese rice wine
¼ cup cider vinegar
2 Tbs low sodium soy sauce
1 cake firm tofu cut into thin strips
1 Ttbs cornstarch
3 beaten egg whites
6 minced scallions
Pepper to taste
½ tsp sesame oil

Place dried mushrooms in a small bowl. Heat 2 cups of the water to boiling. Pour over the mushrooms. Cover with a plate and let stand for about 30 minutes. Drain mushrooms, squeeze out excess water and save the liquid. Slice the mushrooms.

In a large soup pot combine the remaining water, the mushroom broth and sliced mushrooms. Heat to a gentle boil. Add sherry, vinegar, soy sauce and tofu. Lower heat and simmer for about 10 minutes. Place cornstarch in small bowl. Take about a cup of the liquid and whisk it into the cornstarch. When dissolved, stir mixture back into the soup. Drizzle beaten egg whites into simmering soup. Stirring constantly. Add scallions and pepper. Cook for 3 more minutes. Add sesame oil. Serve.

Gazpacho
Prep Time: 20 minutes
Cook Time: 10 minutes
Serves 4

Nutritional Facts:

Calories-165

Total Fat-8g

Sat Fat-1g

Dietary Fiber-5g

Sugars-13g

Sodium- 184 mg

Total Carbohydrates-22g

Trans Fat-0g

Protein-4g

Cholesterol-0mg

I love this soup in the summer. It's refreshing as a starter or a light lunch and is a good source of dietary fiber, vitamin B6, folate, potassium and copper, and a very good source of vitamin A, vitamin C and vitamin K. It seems to have a lot of sugar, but tomatoes, being fruit, have fructose, a form of sugar. Add a touch of soy cheese grated on top for some extra protein!

Ingredients:

4 cups low sodium tomato juice

½ cup minced sweet onion

2 garlic cloves, minced

1 red pepper, cut small

2 cups diced fresh tomatoes

1 medium cucumber, peeled, seeded and cut small

2 scallions, minced

Juice of ½ lemon

2 tbs red wine vinegar

1 tsp basil

¼ tsp cumin

¼ cup fresh chopped parsley

2 tbs olive oil

Pepper

Cayenne pepper to taste

Combine all ingredients; take ½ out, place in blender and puree on pulse. Add back to original pot of soup. Chill until very cold.

Cucumber Mint Soup

Prep Time: 15 minutes
Cook Time: 3 minutes
Chill time: 3 hours
Serves 4

Nutritional Facts:

Calories-179

Total Fat-2g

Sat Fat-1g

Dietary Fiber-4g

Sugars-18g

Sodium- 198 mg

Total Carbohydrates-27g

Trans Fat-0g

Protein-16g

Cholesterol-4mg

A variation of my Mom's Cold Cucumber Soup (see following), this one has a little more kick to it and is very refreshing on a hot summer day. The sugar content, as you can see, is a little high, as is the sodium. Yogurt has milk sugar and salt and the chicken stock still has some sodium in it. You can try to find a stock with very little salt added. They're out there! It's still a good source of protein, vitamin A, vitamin K, riboflavin, folate, vitamin B12, pantothenic acid, magnesium, potassium, copper and manganese, and a very good source of vitamin C, calcium and phosphorus.

Ingredients:

7 small cucumbers, peeled, halved and seeded
1 garlic clove, minced
2 cups low sodium chicken stock
3 cups plain, non-fat yogurt
1 tsp pepper
1 cup fresh mint leaves
1 tsp lemon juice
3 radishes, chopped well, for garnish

Cut 6 of the cucumbers into one-inch pieces. Cut the last one into ¼ inch cubes. Reserve in refrigerator. Put the 6 cucumbers and garlic in a food processor and puree for 30 seconds. Add stock, yogurt, pepper, ¾ cup mint leaves and lemon juice. Process until smooth.

Chop remaining mint and fold into soup. Chill, covered, for 3 hours. When serving, ladle soup into bowl, garnish with radish and reserved diced cucumber.

"Good manners: The noise you don't make when you're eating soup."
Bennett Cerf, humorist, publisher (1898-1971)

Cold Cream of Cucumber Soup
Prep Time: 15 minutes
Cook Time: 30 minutes
Chill Time: 2 hours
Serves 4

Nutritional Facts:

Calories-87

Total Fat-2g

Sat Fat: 1g

Dietary Fiber-2g

Sugars-3g

Sodium-75 mg

Total Carbohydrates-12g

Trans Fat-0g

Protein-6g

Cholesterol-0mg

My Mom made this a lot when I was growing up. It was great on a hot summer day. I just made the chicken broth low sodium and used cooking spray instead of regular oil. It's great with a sandwich. This soup is a good source of vitamin C, vitamin K, phosphorus, potassium, copper and manganese, and a very good source of niacin.

Ingredients:

2 large cucumbers, peeled and sliced

Pam spray

1 onion, sliced

3 TBS flour

4 cups low sodium chicken broth

2 tsp chopped dill

2 tsp chopped chives

Pepper to taste

Sauté sliced onion and cucumber in Pam cooking spray for about 10 minutes. Sift the flour over the cucumber and gradually add 2 cups of chicken broth. Add pepper to taste. Cook vegetables on low heat for 15 more minutes. Turn mixture into a blender or food processor and blend for about 15 seconds or until soup is smooth. Pour soup into large container and add 2 more cups of chicken broth. Chill in 'fridge for 2 hours. When serving, garnish with dill and chives.

Broccoli Soup
Prep Time: 5 minutes
Cook Time: 40 minutes
Serves 4

Nutritional Facts:

Calories-109

Total Fat-1g

Sat Fat-0g

Dietary Fiber-5g

Sugars-6g

Sodium- 90g

Total Carbohydrates-20g

Trans Fat-0g

Protein-8g

Cholesterol-0g

I love this soup hot or cold. I learned this easy recipe from the head of the household staff of a wealthy shipping magnate. She also happened to also be the part time chef. Her recipes are all like this, easy, but with big flavor. It's a great source of fiber, vitamin A; it has lots of vitamin C, riboflavin, niacin, vitamin B6 and potassium.

Ingredients:
1 large bunch of broccoli, stalks included
2-3 onions, chopped
4 garlic cloves
3 bay leaves
1 can of low sodium chicken stock
Water to cover

Place all ingredients in large saucepan. Just cover with water and bring to a boil. Simmer until soft. Remove bay leaves. Remove from heat and let cool for about 15 minutes. Pour into Cuisinart or blender and puree. Re-heat to serve.

Chicken Florentine Soup
Prep Time: 25 minutes
Cook Time: 35-40 minutes
Serves 4

Nutritional Facts:

Calories-200

Total Fat-6g

Sat Fat-2g

Dietary Fiber-5g

Sugars-8g

Sodium- 53g

Total Carbohydrates-22g

Trans Fat-0g

Protein-18g

Cholesterol-24g

I made up this recipe up after an afternoon lunch in Aspen. I had just come from skiing with friends to this little, out-of-the-way pub where they had delicious homemade soup. It was a version of this. I asked for the recipe, but the waitress would only list the ingredients by heart. After some experimentation, I came upon this, which is a great one-dish meal on a cold day. Want a little more heartiness? Add a can of low-sodium garbanzo beans. It's a good source of protein, vitamin B6, iron, potassium and a really good source of vitamin A, vitamin C, vitamin K and niacin.

Ingredients:

1 pound Roma tomatoes, peeled and seeded

2 tbsp Smart Balance Butter substitute

1 onion, diced

3 14 oz cans, low sodium chicken broth

4 cups water

3 bay leaves

1 tbs dried oregano or 2 tsp fresh oregano

¼ cup fresh parsley leaves, chopped

Pepper

1 ½ cups fresh spinach, chopped

1 28 oz. can tomato puree

4 cloves of garlic, minced

2 chicken breasts, cubed

¼ cup fresh basil, chopped

Pepper chicken breasts. Heat Smart Balance in skillet and add chicken. Sauté each side for 3-4 minutes. Take out and put on the side in bowl. Add garlic and onion to skillet and sauté until soft. Add tomatoes and cook down, about 5 to 8 minutes. Add puree, chicken broth and water. Stir. Add all other ingredients. Simmer for another 15 minutes. Serve.

Mom's Garbage Soup
Prep Time: 40 minutes
Cook Time: 2 hours
Serves 10

Nutritional Facts: Meat version

Calories-300

Total Fat-5g

Sat Fat-2g

Dietary Fiber-11g

Sugars-10g

Sodium- 213g

Total Carbohydrates-34g

Trans Fat-0g

Protein-36g

Cholesterol-39g

Nutritional Facts: Vegetarian version

Calories-181

Total Fat-2g

Sat Fat-2g

Dietary Fiber-11g

Sugars-9g

Sodium- 129g

Total Carbohydrates-34g

Trans Fat-0g

Protein-36g

Cholesterol-0g

This is the most complicated recipe in the book. I've included it because, overall, it's a pretty healthy soup that can double as a one-dish meal. I went home and actually made this with Mom in the kitchen I grew up in. Of course, this automatically means I reverted to being 14 years old. And evidently, I still don't know what I'm doing in the kitchen, either.

It took all of 2 ½ minutes of cutting vegetables for me to mess up. I started slicing the leek, like I usually do. "NO! NO! NOT LIKE THAT!" I hear from behind me. Evidently, I was supposed to cut the tough ends off, cut ½ way up the stalk and spread it out so the dirt is easier to clean out. Whoops. I just cut the end off and sliced the thing into a colander and ran water over it. Still looked clean to me! Then, I volunteered to peel and cut the turnips. BUT, I cut them too small. Silly me, thinking that each piece should actually fit INSIDE your mouth. Nope, I was supposed to cut them just big enough that you have to cut it with your spoon after it's in your plate.

After that, I just watched.

But it was worth it. It's a wonderful, filling and healthy meal with lots of fiber, Protein, Vitamin K, B vitamins, Phosphorus, Potassium, Zinc, Manganese and Selenium, and a really good source of Vitamin A and Vitamin C.

One more thing to remember; NEVER eat this on the same day you make it. Any good cook knows the flavor in this kind of soup melds overnight. Mom's rules! And as we all know…Moms rule. I love you, Mom.

Meat Version-Add this to vegetarian version:
2-2 ½ lbs Short Ribs

5-6 Rosy bones (ask your butcher…he'll know what they are. Basically, they're soup bones with no marrow.)

2 qts of low sodium beef broth

Vegetarian Version-

2 qts low sodium vegetable broth (sub for beef broth)

2 lbs green cabbage, chopped well

3 parsnips, cut into bite sized pieces

1 leek, sliced thin

2 med turnips, cut in bit sized pieces

3 carrots, cut in 1" slices or 1 small bag, leaving them whole

3 ribs celery, cut in bite sized pieces

½ c fresh peas

1/3 lb string beans, chopped in 1" pieces

8 oz button mushrooms, quartered

2 medium onions, one chopped and one peeled and whole

1 bunch dill

1 bunch Italian parsley

1 28 oz can diced tomatoes (or a few soft tomatoes chopped up)

4 cloves of garlic-minced

½ cup lentils, cleaned and rinsed

Pepper to taste

Garlic powder to taste

Optional

1 celery knob (Peel and keep whole. Add at the same time as string beans. Remove when soup is done)

1 parsley root (Peel and cup up. Add at the same time as parsnips)

1/3 cup pearl barley (Add with carrots)

1 medium potato (Add with celery)

Meat version start:

In a large stockpot, at least 12 quarts in size put the beef and bones in 1 quart of water. Boil for about 45 minutes. Skim the top of the water until clear. Add stock and continue with the vegetarian version.

When the entire recipe is done, turn off the light and take the meat and bones out of the pot. According to Mom, you should put it in a separate container. See, if, by chance, you don't eat this immediately…or within a couple of days, it won't ruin the rest of the soup, which will last a whole week. Clever, isn't she?

Vegetarian Start:

Put stock in 12-quart stockpot. Bring to a boil. Add carrots, whole onion, parsnips and turnips. Stir. Cook for 15 minutes over medium heat. Add string beans, leek and cabbage. Stir, cook for 15 minutes. Add celery and onion. Cook 10 minutes more. Wrap the bunch of dill and parsley together with white thread and knot. Add to soup. Cook another 5 minutes. Add mushrooms, potato and lentils, tomato and fresh garlic and peas. Stir. Add pepper and garlic powder to taste. Mom occasionally adds a tsp of Ms. Dash original spices.

Stir. Cook for another 15-20 minutes. Serve.

Zucchini
and Carrots

Mushrooms in Lemon Marinade

Side Dishes

I was thinking about calling this section *"Dishes to Eat if you're a Vegetarian, Vegan or if you Just want a Little Nosh."*

But, I figured that was too long.

Why do people NEED side dishes, anyway? Do you think they were invented out of boredom? Perhaps people didn't like eating just ONE dish, but had a favorite, so the other dishes became smaller, and fit on the "side" of the big dish.

In that case, why wouldn't you just call them BIG dishes and SMALL dishes?

And most of us eat on round dishes, do we not? So, where exactly IS the side? Should we really put them on top? Or would you put them on a small plate to the side of the big plate?

The Merriam-Webster dictionary tells us that a side dish is: *a food served separately along with a main course.*

Hold it. Separately? Along with? Well is it separate or is it along with? Isn't that an oxy-moron-- like Jumbo Shrimp? Perhaps it's like I thought before…separately on a *little* plate on the side of another *big* plate of food.

Nowadays, cooks are getting so creative with their side dishes, there's no need for a main course! I mean, if there were no main dish, would the meal be considered tapas? Samples of everything? Kind of a tease, then, don't you think? What happens if you REALLY like one of the dishes? Does that one then become the MAIN course, since that's your favorite? Perhaps you should "MAINLY eat this dish, but you can have a taste of these others on the side…as long as you *mainly* eat *this* dish."

Well, however you choose to serve them, the recipes in this section are very versatile. You can make many of these dishes with some brown rice, like the stewed beans with kale or the oven-baked mixed vegetables. Personally, I love the ratatouille over a baked potato when I feel like going vegetarian. I prefer my dishes a little spicy, too, so I often add some red pepper flakes to these dishes. Except, perhaps for the Mushrooms in Lemon Marinade, they're all hearty enough to take a little added spice. Any of these dishes will make your favorite vegetarian very happy, so you can always double a recipe to have enough for a main course or use them as is to add a little pizzazz to a broiled steak or roast chicken…

Stewed Beans with Kale
Prep Time: 20 minutes
Cook Time: 20 minutes
Serves 4

Nutritional Facts:

Calories-181

Total Fat-2g

Sat Fat-0g

Dietary Fiber-8g

Sugars-3g

Sodium- 371g

Total Carbohydrates-35g

Trans Fat-0g

Protein-10g

Cholesterol-0g

Kale is an incredibly healthy green. This is a very hearty side dish. It's very low in saturated fat and cholesterol; it's a good source of fiber, protein, vitamin B6 and iron. It's a very good source of vitamin A, vitamin C, vitamin K and manganese.

Ingredients:
Olive oil spray

2 small shallots, finely chopped

3 cloves of garlic, minced

1 pound of kale, stems removed and torn into pieces.

Juice from one lemon

1 packet of stevia

2 bay leaves

¼ teaspoon red pepper flakes

1 14.5 can low sodium vegetable broth

1 28 oz. can low sodium diced tomatoes, undrained

1 15 oz. can white or pinto beans

Black pepper to taste

Spray a large pot with olive oil spray. Heat over medium heat. Add shallots and cook for 4 minutes. Add garlic and greens and cook, until greens start to wilt, stirring occasionally for about 5 minutes. Add 1 tablespoon lemon juice, stevia, bay leaf, red pepper flakes, broth and tomatoes and their juices. Bring to a boil. Reduce the heat and simmer for 15 minutes. Add beans and cook 5 more minutes. Remove the bay leaf. Season with pepper and remaining lemon juice.

Fun Food Tip: Freeze leftover wine in ice cube trays. Use them in casseroles and sauces.

Zucchini and Carrots with Fresh Mint or Parsley
Prep Time: 15 minutes
Cook Time: 15 minutes
Serves 4

Nutritional Facts:

Calories-67
Total Fat-4g
Sat Fat-1g
Dietary Fiber-2g
Sugars-4g

Sodium- 64g
Total Carbohydrates-24g
Trans Fat-0g
Protein-2g
Cholesterol-0g

OK, I admit it. I'm not a big cooked carrot fan. But, this recipe is good...the mint cuts the sweetness of the carrots, as does the pepper. It's very low in cholesterol and a good source of fiber. It has lots of vitamin A, vitamin C, vitamin K and vitamin B6.

Ingredients:

3 carrots or about ½ pound small ones, trimmed and scraped
2 zucchini, about ¾ pound, ends trimmed
Pam butter spray
Pepper
3 tsp freshly chopped mint or parsley
Smart Balance Butter Substitute

Cut the large carrots into rounds if using those. Cut the zucchini into 1½-inch logs, then quarter the logs into sticks to match the small carrots. Spray Pam onto large skillet. Add carrots and pepper. Cover and cook about 3 to 5 minutes or until half cooked. Add zucchini and cover. Shake skillet occasionally. Cook 4 minutes more or until veggies are crisp/tender. Sprinkle with mint or parsley and more pepper, if desired. Place in a bowl and add 1 tbsp Smart Balance on top. Mix in as it melts.

Yellow Tomatoes in Balsamic Vinaigrette
Prep Time: 25 minutes
Cook Time: 5 minutes
Serves 4

Nutritional Facts:
Calories-103

Total Fat-2g

Sat Fat-0g

Dietary Fiber-3g

Sugars-8g

Sodium- 29mg

Total Carbohydrates-19g

Trans Fat-0g

Protein-2g

Cholesterol-0mg

This dish has some very interesting spices in it. It's low in saturated fat and sodium, has no cholesterol and its got fiber, iron and potassium. It's a great source of vitamin A, C, K and manganese.

Ingredients:
½ cup thinly sliced green onions
1 Tbs minced and seeded jalapeno pepper
8 medium yellow tomatoes cut into wedges (about 2 ½ pounds)
Pam olive oil spray
¼ c grated fresh ginger
1 tbs cumin
1 tbs fresh cracked pepper
2 tsp paprika
1 tsp ground tumeric
4 garlic cloves, minced
¾ cup balsamic vinegar
2 packages stevia sugar substitute

Combine onions, jalapeno pepper and tomatoes in a large bowl. Spray oil in large saucepan over medium-high heat. Add ginger, cumin, pepper, paprika, tumeric and garlic. Sauté 1 minute. Add vinegar, stevia and stir. Bring to a boil and cook for 1 minute. Pour spice mixture over tomato mixture. Toss to coat. Serve at room temp. Serves 6-8.

Roasted Red Peppers
Prep Time: 10 minutes
Cook Time: 30 minutes
Serves 8

Nutritional Facts:

Calories-34

Total Fat-0g

Sat Fat-0g

Dietary Fiber-3g

Sugars-5g

Sodium- 5mg

Total Carbohydrates-8g

Trans Fat-0g

Protein-1g

Cholesterol-0mg

Now this is the low calorie version, which is low sodium, a good source of thiamin, riboflavin and niacin. It's very good source of fiber, vitamin A, C, E and K, vitamin B6 and potassium. If you want the not-as-low calorie, with a different flavor, spray a little Pam olive oil on them before you put them in under the broiler and instead of lemon juice, sprinkle with balsamic vinegar. I also like to put the leftovers in a couple of tablespoons of the vinegar. Leave it overnight and the flavors marry up really well!

Ingredients:

6 Red bell peppers

Fresh lemon juice from 1 lemon

Ground pepper to taste

Preheat the broiler. Halve peppers lengthwise and take out seeds. Put them skin side up on the broiling pan. Broil them 2-3" from the heat. When skin blackens (check frequently), turn peppers until the skin is black all over. Using tongs or a wide spatula, transfer peppers to a plastic bag and seal with a twisty. Let peppers cool in bag for about 20 minutes. Remove from bag and peel off skin. Place peppers in a shallow dish, drizzle them with lemon juice and sprinkle with black pepper. Serve warm or room temperature.

Ratatouille

Prep Time: 35 minutes
Cook Time: 45 minutes
Serves 4

Nutritional Facts:

Calories-95

Total Fat-1g

Sat Fat-0g

Dietary Fiber-8g

Sugars-9g

Sodium- 22mg

Total Carbohydrates-21g

Trans Fat-0g

Protein-4g

Cholesterol-0mg

    I love this dish. There are lots of variations on it and you can use your imagination. Have extra broccoli left? Throw it in!! Use different kinds of mushrooms to add earthier flavor. It's very low fat and low in sodium. It's a good source of magnesium, thiamin, riboflavin, niacin and copper. This has a lot of fiber, vitamin A, vitamin C, vitamin K, vitamin B6 and potassium. Vegans will love this dish as a main course, too!

Ingredients:

2 ½ pounds eggplant-cut into cubes

7 sprigs of fresh dill, tough stems removed

2 ½ pounds zucchini, sliced in ¼" slices

1 ¼ pounds onion, peeled and sliced

3 green and red peppers cut into 1" pieces

3 cloves of garlic put through garlic press

6 sprigs of fresh parsley

1 tsp dried oregano

5-6 large mushrooms

1 lb fresh ripe plum tomatoes

6-8 Tbs distilled white vinegar

Ground pepper

    Place all of the ingredients in one large pot. Mix contents to distribute seasonings. Cover and cook over low heat, just below simmer for about 45 minutes. When all veggies are soft, serve. Opt: add soy Parmesan cheese.

Oven-Baked Mixed Vegetables
Prep Time: 25 minutes
Cook Time: 1 hour
Serves 6

Nutritional Facts:

Calories-74

Total Fat-1g

Sat Fat-0g

Dietary Fiber-6g

Sugars-7g

Sodium- 10mg

Total Carbohydrates-16g

Trans Fat-0g

Protein-3g

Cholesterol-0mg

If you're a vegan, add some brown rice for a great main dish. It has no saturated fat, is very low in sodium and gives you pantothenic acid, iron, copper and selenium. It's a great source of fiber, vitamins A, C and K, riboflavin, niacin, vitamin B6, potassium and folate.

Ingredients:

1 small firm eggplant, cut into 2" cubes

3 large red bell peppers, cored, seeded and cut into 1" strips

2 medium sized onions, quartered

10 oz small fresh white mushrooms or Portobello mushrooms cut into 2" pieces

4 garlic cloves, peeled

Pepper to taste

2 Tbs dried oregano

Pam olive oil spray

1 c cold water

2 tbs chopped parsley

¼ cup red wine vinegar

Pre-heat oven to 350 degrees. Place veggies in one layer in a large baking pan. Spray with Pam. Season with pepper and oregano. Add water and cover pan tightly with aluminum foil. Bake 20 to 25 minutes. Discard foil and stir. Bake 30 minutes longer, stirring once or twice. With slotted spoon, transfer veggies to a bowl. Add ½ cup cooking broth, parsley and red wine vinegar. Toss. Serve warm or room temp.

Mushrooms in Lemon Marinade
Prep Time: 20 minutes
Cook Time: 6 minutes plus one hour
Serves 4

Nutritional Facts:

Calories-43

Total Fat-1g

Sat Fat-0g

Dietary Fiber-2g

Sugars-2g

Sodium- 9mg

Total Carbohydrates-8g

Trans Fat-0g

Protein-3g

Cholesterol-0mg

One of the many things I love about mushrooms is that the varieties add tons of flavor to dishes, but it's like they're made of air! They don't add calories, fat, sodium… anything! The nutritional facts show that well! This recipe is, however, a nice source of fiber, thiamine, vitamin B6, folate, iron and zinc. There's also a lot of vitamin C, vitamin K, riboflavin, niacin and potassium! You get so much for so little. Nice return for your money, I'd say!

Ingredients:

1 pound small mushrooms

Olive oil spray

3 cloves of garlic, minced

1 tbs minced fresh basil

2 tbs minced fresh parsley

Juice of 1 lemon

2 tbs chicken broth

Ground pepper to taste

Wash mushrooms and slice off and discard stems. In a non-stick skillet, spray olive oil to completely cover bottom. Over medium, high heat, sauté garlic for one minute. Add mushrooms, broth and herbs and sauté for 4 minutes, stirring occasionally. Add lemon juice, toss well and cook for one more minute. Pour mushrooms and juice into a serving bowl. Set aside for at least one hour. Serve hot or at room temperature. Serves 4.

Fun Food Tip: To get the most juice out of fresh lemons, bring them to room temperature and roll them under your palm against the kitchen counter before squeezing.

"We are living in a world today where lemonade is made from artificial flavors and furniture polish is made from real lemons."

Alfred E. Newman

Marinated Zucchini
Prep Time: 5 minutes
Cook Time: 10 minutes
Serves 4

Nutritional Facts:

Calories-37
Total Fat-1g
Sat Fat-0g
Dietary Fiber-2g
Sugars-3g

Sodium- 16mg
Total Carbohydrates-7g
Trans Fat-0g
Protein-2g
Cholesterol-0mg

I'm not a huge fan of zucchini by itself, to be honest. I make it a lot with tomato sauce. Anything's good with tomato sauce! But this recipe has so much flavor it's terrific! The zucchini has a lot of fiber, vitamin A, thiamine, magnesium, phosphorus and copper. It's also got a ton of vitamin C, vitamin K, vitamin B6 and riboflavin.

Ingredients:

3 medium zucchini
Olive oil spray
4 cloves of garlic, minced
1 TBS fresh basil
1 TBS fresh red wine or balsamic vinegar
Dash of pepper

Wash and dry the zucchini. Cut diagonally into wedges. In a large skillet, spray the olive oil spray just enough to coat the bottom of the skillet. Over medium-high heat, quickly fry the zucchini until golden on the outside and tender on the inside. You may need a few batches to do this. Drain on paper towels. Lower the heat and sauté the garlic, stirring constantly until just turning tan. Put the zucchini in a bowl and sprinkle with basil, vinegar, pepper and garlic. Stir carefully and set aside to marinate. Should be served at room temperature. Can be kept for 4 days in refrigerator.

Fun Food Tip: White vinegar heals bruises. Soak a cotton ball in white vinegar and apply it to the bruise for one hour. The vinegar reduces the blueness and speeds up the healing process.

Italian Pepper Sauté

Prep Time: 15 minutes
Cook Time: 25 minutes
Serves 4

Nutritional Facts:

Calories-150

Total Fat-7g

Sat Fat-1g

Dietary Fiber-5g

Sugars-12g

Sodium- 19mg

Total Carbohydrates-21g

Trans Fat-0g

Protein-3g

Cholesterol-0mg

I also use this on meatloaf…or mix a bit IN meatloaf…especially turkey or tofu. It keeps the loaf moist and flavorful. This freezes very well, too. If you'd like to, you can cut more fat and calories by substituting spray oil for the olive oil. In this case, however, it would affect the taste. Live a little. Splurge on the amount of olive oil. It's good for you. This has a lot of fiber, vitamin E, vitamin K, potassium and it's a great source of vitamin A and vitamin C.

Ingredients:

3 red peppers

2 yellow or orange peppers

2 or 3 sweet onions

2 tbs olive oil

1c undrained canned plum tomatoes, chopped

2 tbs red wine or balsamic vinegar

Black pepper to taste

Slice peppers and onions into strips. Heat oil on medium heat in large skillet. Add peppers and onions and sauté, stirring frequently for about 13 minutes or until tender and light brown.

Stir the tomatoes and vinegar into the pepper mix and cook for about 5 minutes. Add black pepper. Serve hot.

Haricots Verts with Garlic
Prep Time: 5 minutes
Cook Time: 10 minutes
Serves 4

Nutritional Facts:

Calories-35
Total Fat-2g
Sat Fat-0g
Dietary Fiber-2g
Sugars-1g

Sodium- 15mg
Total Carbohydrates-5g
Trans Fat-0g
Protein-1g
Cholesterol-0mg

This is a nice, simple side dish. It's low in sodium, has folate, iron and magnesium and it's a very good source of fiber, vitamin A, vitamin C, vitamin K and manganese.

Ingredients:

2 cups haricots verts. Cleaned green beans can be substituted.
1 tsp Smart Balance Butter Substitute
Cooking spray
Pepper to taste
2 garlic cloves, minced

Cook beans in boiling water 2 minutes. Drain and plunge beans into ice water. Drain. Melt Smart Balance in a small non-stick skillet coated with cooking spray over medium heat. Add garlic. Cook for 1 minute. Add haricot verts and pepper. Cook another 2 minutes. Serve.

Green Beans Provencal

Prep Time: 25 minutes
Cook Time: 45 minutes
Serves 4

Nutritional Facts:

Calories-164

Total Fat-4g

Sat Fat-1g

Dietary Fiber-8g

Sugars-3g

Sodium- 271mg

Total Carbohydrates-26g

Trans Fat-0g

Protein-5g

Cholesterol-0mg

The olives make this slightly higher in fat and calories, but olive oil is so good for you, and this dish is such a great source of fiber, don't even worry about it. It has a lot of vitamin K, folate, iron, potassium and copper. It's a great source of vitamin A, vitamin C and manganese.

Ingredients:
1 pound fresh green beans, cleaned
Olive oil spray
1 large onion, coarsely chopped
5 cloves of garlic, finely chopped
4 large tomatoes, peeled, seeded and coarsely chopped
½ cup dry white wine
½ cup pitted black olives
1 tbs lemon juice
2 Tbs coarsely ground black pepper

Bring a saucepan of water to boil. Add beans. Simmer until just tender, about 3 minutes. Rinse under cold water, drain, rinse again and drain again. Set beans aside.

Spray Olive Oil in a large skillet over medium heat. Add onions and garlic. Cook for 5 minutes. Add tomatoes and wine and cook another 20 minutes. Toss in olives and reserved beans. Heat another 3 minutes. Sprinkle with lemon juice and pepper. Toss and serve.

Cherry Tomatoes with Garlic and Parsley

Prep Time: 5 minutes
Cook Time: 2 minutes
Serves 4

Nutritional Facts:

Calories-56
Total Fat-2g
Sat Fat-0g
Dietary Fiber-2g
Sugars-4g

Sodium- 21mg
Total Carbohydrates-10g
Trans Fat-0g
Protein-2g
Cholesterol-0mg

This dish is great with Italian style dishes or to dress up a plain main course. It's very low in sodium, has lots of fiber, thiamine, riboflavin, niacin, vitamin B6, folate iron and copper. It's a really good source of vitamin A, vitamin C, vitamin K and potassium.

Ingredients:
24 red, ripe cherry tomatoes
Olive oil spray
1 tsp finely chopped garlic
2 Tbsp finely chopped parsley

Remove stems from tomatoes. Spray skillet and heat on medium/high heat. Place tomatoes in one layer in the pan. Cook, shaking the skillet for about 1-1 ½ minutes. Do not overcook or the skins will split. Sprinkle with garlic, toss briefly and sprinkle with parsley. Serve.

Fun Food Tip: Can't open your jars? Try using latex dishwashing gloves. They give a non-slip grip that makes opening jars easy.

Broiled Tomatoes
Prep Time: 20 minutes
Cook Time: 5 minutes
Serves 4

Nutritional Facts:

Calories-54

Total Fat-0g

Sat Fat-0g

Dietary Fiber-2g

Sugars-4g

Sodium- 17mg

Total Carbohydrates-10g

Trans Fat-0g

Protein-2g

Cholesterol-0mg

A mainstay in any "what can I make quickly?" repertoire. It's a good source of fiber, iron and a very good source of vitamin A, vitamin c and potassium.

Ingredients:
2 ripe tomatoes
Pam olive oil spray
Fresh pepper to taste
2 cloves of garlic, peeled

Preheat the broiler. Spray Pam inside a baking dish. Cut tomatoes in half and arrange them in dish. Sprinkle with pepper. Cut the garlic into small, thin slices. Stud the tomato halves with slivers and spray with Pam. Place under broiler about 5 minutes or until garlic slivers start to burn. Remove from broiler and discard garlic. Serve immediately.

Braised Mixed Bell Peppers
Prep Time: 25 minutes
Cook Time: 45 minutes
Serves 4

Nutritional Facts:

Calories-116
Total Fat-2g
Sat Fat-0g
Dietary Fiber-6g
Sugars-5g

Sodium- 35mg
Total Carbohydrates-24g
Trans Fat-0g
Protein-5g
Cholesterol-0mg

I love peppers. Sometimes I'll broil some chicken breasts and smother this on top as a sauce. It's a great dish to double or triple and freeze for whenever you need it! It's a good source of protein, fiber, vitamin A, vitamin C and vitamin B6.

Ingredients:

1 green pepper
2 red peppers
1 yellow pepper
1 orange pepper
1 onion, peeled
3 garlic cloves, peeled
Olive oil spray
4 very ripe tomatoes
1 tbs fresh chopped oregano
Black pepper to taste
2/3 c low sodium chicken broth

Remove the seeds from the bell peppers and cut into thin strips. Slice the onion into rings and chop the garlic finely. Spray skillet and heat over medium heat. Cook peppers, onions and garlic for 5-10 minutes or until soft and lightly browned. Stir often. Make a cross on top of the tomatoes, then place in a bowl and cover with boiling water. Let it stand for 2 minutes. Drain, then remove the skins and seeds, and chop the flesh into cubes. Add the tomatoes and oregano to peppers and onion mixture. Season with black pepper.

Cover the skillet and bring to a boil. Simmer for about 30 minutes or until tender. Add chicken stock after about 15 minutes. Serve hot or cold.

Garbanzos with Spinach
Prep Time: 15 minutes
Cook Time: 20 minutes
Serves 8

Nutritional Facts:

Calories-141

Total Fat-3g

Sat Fat-0g

Dietary Fiber-10g

Sugars-7g

Sodium- 90mg

Total Carbohydrates-38g

Trans Fat-0g

Protein-12g

Cholesterol-0mg

I discovered a version of this recipe while researching a dish to make for my monthly "pot luck" dinner gathering. Everyone cooks REALLY well there, so it's more like "gourmet pot luck." There's a different theme every month and this one was for Spanish food. It's a great side dish, but I've eaten it as a vegetarian entrée over brown rice. I love the touch of lemon combined with the spiciness of the red pepper flakes. I add a little more of these for more zest. There's lots of fiber and protein and it's very high in Vitamin A. This recipe will keep you full for quite some time!

Ingredients:

Pam cooking spray

1 ½ c finely chopped onion

½ tsp red pepper flakes

5 garlic cloves, minced

1 tsp ground cumin

1 c warm water

1/8 c dry breadcrumbs, plain

2 tbs dry sherry

¼ tsp saffron threads

2 15oz. cans of organic garbanzo beans, drained (as low sodium as you can find)

2 10oz packages of fresh spinach

1 tbs fresh parsley, chopped

1 tbs fresh lemon juice

1 tsp fresh ground pepper

Spray Pam in a 4 or 6 quart pot over medium high heat. Add chopped onion and stir for about 2 minutes. Add red pepper flakes and garlic. Stir for another minute. Add cumin. Stir. Add water, breadcrumbs, sherry saffron and garbanzos. Stir until it starts to thicken. Add the spinach a handful at a time and as each one wilts, add more. Take pot off the heat. Stir in parsley, lemon juice and lots of black pepper. Serve as a side dish

Fish Fillets
in Foil

Light Shrimp
Scampi

Main Courses

Dinner is the "principal act of the day that can only be carried out in a worthy manner by people of wit and humor; for it is not sufficient just to eat at dinner. One has to talk with a calm and discreet gaiety. The conversation must sparkle like the rubies in the entremets wines, it must be delightfully suave with the sweetmeats of the dessert, and become very profound with the coffee."
Alexandre Dumas (1802-1870)

(Obviously, he never had dinner with kids who were late for soccer practice)

Families don't sit down together for dinner anymore. They're always running to volleyball practice, piano lessons, club events, and a number of additional excuses for not staying for dinner. How did that happen? When I was a kid, we had dinner together just about every single night and all 3 of us kids participated in sports, played instruments and were pretty busy. (I took piano lessons. Please don't ask me to play anything…ever. You'll be truly sorry.). If you want to bring your family together so that you might be able to remember what each other actually looks like without checking the pictures in your wallet, then you'll want to attract them with something to make them want to eat dinner. I think when a dish is the center of attention; it should be fun and interesting…not basic and boring. They also need to be quick and easy.

Studies have shown that most women have a repertoire of about 15 dishes they make over and over again. Let's see. Since there are 365 days a year, each dish would be made about 24 times a year. Oy! I'm bored already. And if I'm bored (and I don't even live at your house), imagine how your family feels! How hard is it to try something new? All you have to do is take time to READ a new recipe then shop for the ingredients, right? You have to shop for food, anyway! I rest my case.

With this in mind, the recipes in this section are probably different from what you've been cooking, and you can make them without needing all kinds of weird spices you have to mail order from Bolivia. So, if you make every single recipe in this section, you'll have enough for over a month…and that doesn't even include leftovers! This means you'd only cook each recipe 10 or 11 times this year. See? Your life is less boring already!

This chapter is dedicated to all families, in the hope that it might make it easier to gather them together for a great tasting, healthy meal. If the kids look forward to dinner at home, there's a pretty good chance you'll actually SEE them before they graduate and won't be hearing quite as many excuses as to why they can't stick around for dinner. They may even start having their friends come over!

Veal Stew with Tomatoes and Balsamic Vinegar
Prep Time: 15 minutes
Cook Time: 1 hour, 40 minutes
Serves 8

Nutritional Facts:

Calories-321

Total Fat-10g

Sat Fat-2g

Dietary Fiber-1g

Sugars-3g

Sodium- 275mg

Total Carbohydrates-7g

Trans Fat-0g

Protein-47g

Cholesterol-190mg

I used to make this a lot when I lived in Colorado. It's warm, hearty and great with crusty bread to sop up the gravy. Hey, when it's minus 2 outside, you don't care about how lean you are, just how you can stay warm! Now, I just pair this with some steamed broccoli and the gravy makes it taste terrific! (OK…OK…I know…not as good as crusty bread)   It's a great source of protein and niacin, too!

Ingredients:

2 tbs olive oil

3 lbs veal for stew (lean)

¾ c finely chopped onion

1 cup veal or beef stock

4 tbs balsamic vinegar

1 ½ cups finely chopped ripe plum tomatoes

1 ½ tsp fresh rosemary leaves or 1 tsp dried

1 tsp fresh garlic, chopped

Pepper to taste

Heat 1 Tbs oil in heavy flameproof casserole. Add veal in batches and lightly brown over high heat. As pieces are browned, remove them and set aside. Add remaining olive oil to casserole and the onion; lower the heat and lightly brown onion. Stir in stock, vinegar and tomatoes. Simmer for 5 minutes. Add rosemary, garlic, and pepper. Return meat to casserole and stir. Cover and simmer for 1 hour until meat is tender. Serve.

Fun Food Tip: To keep potatoes from budding, place an apple in the bag with them. (Because, cooking low carb, you need them to last longer, don't you?)

Casserole of Lamb and Eggplant
Prep Time: 20 minutes
Cook Time: 20 plus 15 minutes bake time
Serves 4

Nutritional Facts:
Calories-297
Total Fat-9g
Sat Fat-0g
Sugars-6g

Sodium- 200mg
Total Carbohydrates-10g
Protein-40g
Cholesterol-116mg

This dish has a Mediterranean flair and is hot and sweet at the same time. You can also substitute ground turkey, but increase the spices a bit as lamb has more flavor. This is a good source of riboflavin, niacin and vitamin B6. It has a ton of protein, vitamin B12 and zinc.

Ingredients:
1 large eggplant, about 1 ½ pounds
Pam olive oil spray
2 tsp minced garlic
Fresh pepper to taste
½ tsp ground cinnamon
1 bay leaf
1 dried hot red pepper
4 cups (28 oz can) tomatoes in tomato paste
Soy Parmesan Cheese
1 ½ lbs ground lamb
1 medium onion-sliced

Pre-heat oven to 425 degrees. Peel eggplant. Cut eggplant lengthwise into 1" thick slices. Cut slices into strips about 1" wide and the strips into cubes. Spray Pam into deep casserole dish and add heat over med-high heat. Add onion and garlic. Cook until onion is wilted. Add lamb, chopping down with spoon to break up any lumps. Add eggplant and cook, stirring often, about 5 minutes. Add pepper, cinnamon, bay leaf, hot pepper and tomatoes. Cook, stirring for 5 minutes. Spoon mixture into a baking dish. Sprinkle with Parmesan cheese and bake for 15 minutes.

Boneless Loin Of Lamb with Tarragon
Prep Time: 10 minutes
Cook Time: 20-25 minutes
Serves 2

Nutritional Facts:

Calories-352

Total Fat-11g

Sat Fat-3g

Dietary Fiber-0g

Sugars-0g

Sodium- 251 mg

Total Carbohydrates-4g

Trans Fat-0g

Protein-48g

Cholesterol-150mg

I really like lamb. This is a nice way to make it that's an elegant alternative to a rack of lamb. It makes for an intimate, romantic meal, too! It's very high in protein, vitamin B12 and zinc.

Ingredients:
2 skinless, boneless loins of lamb, about ½ lb each

Fresh pepper

Pam buttery spray

2 tbs finely chopped shallots

2 tsp finely chopped tarragon

1/3 cup dry white wine

¼ cup low sodium chicken broth

Sprinkle lamb with pepper to taste. Spray Pam in a large skillet. Over relatively high heat, brown quickly on all sides and cook for about 10 minutes. Remove to a warm platter. Pour fat from skillet and re-spray with Pam. Add shallots and cook briefly, stirring, until soft. Add tarragon and wine. Cook until wine is reduced by half. Add broth and cook for 1 minute. Add any juices that have accumulated around lamb. Pour sauce over lamb.

"When the waitress puts the dinner on the table the old men look at the dinner. The young men look at the waitress."

Gelett Burgess *'Look Eleven Years Younger'* (1937).

Pork Chops Pizzaiola

Prep Time: 15 minutes
Cook Time: 1 hour
Serves 4

Nutritional Facts:

Calories-406
Total Fat-17g
Sat Fat-5g
Dietary Fiber-3g
Sugars-6g

Sodium- 119
Total Carbohydrates-9g
Trans Fat-0g
Protein-52g
Cholesterol-125mg

This is also nice sprinkled with a little Parmesan. It's low in sodium and carbohydrates, a great source of protein, vitamin c and thiamine. Keep those chops lean!

Ingredients:

2 cups canned tomatoes
Pepper to taste
4 - ½ pound loin pork chops
Pam olive oil spray
2 teaspoons chopped garlic
1 ½ cups thinly sliced mushrooms
1 ½ green or red pepper cut into 1" pieces
½ cup dry white wine
1 teaspoon oregano

Put the tomatoes in a saucepan and bring to a boil. Lower heat and simmer stirring occasionally, for about 5 minutes. Add pepper and put aside. Sprinkle pork with pepper. Spray large skillet with Pam and brown chops on both sides, about 5 minutes to a side. Add garlic, mushrooms and peppers. Cover and cook about 5 minutes. Add wine, tomatoes and oregano. Add pepper to taste. Cover and cook about 35 minutes.

Grilled Pork Medallions with Herb Marinade
Prep Time: 30 minutes
Cook Time: 6-8 minutes
Serves 4

Nutritional Facts:

Calories-323

Total Fat-18g

Sat Fat-5g

Dietary Fiber-1g

Sugars-3g

Sodium- 78mg

Total Carbohydrates-1g

Trans Fat-0g

Protein-37g

Cholesterol-94mg

This marinade works well with pork or chicken. Experiment with different flavored vinegars! The dish is low in carbs and is a good source of niacin, vitamin B6, and phosphorus with a lot of protein, thiamine and selenium.

Ingredients:

1 ½ lbs boneless loin of pork

Pam olive oil spray

1/8 cup olive oil

2 Tbs red wine vinegar

Fresh ground pepper

1 tsp chopped fresh rosemary

1 tsp dried cumin

Preheat Charcoal or gas grill. Cut the pork into 8 even slices. Put each slice on a flat surface, cover with clear plastic wrap and pound slightly with flat mallet. Put oil, vinegar and pepper in a flat dish and stir. Add rosemary and cumin. Stir again. Add pork slices. Turn them over in the marinade. Cover with foil and let sit for 15 minutes. Add medallions to grill and cook 3-4 minutes on one side. Flip and cook another 2-3 minutes.

Stir-Fried Pea Shoots and Shiitakes with Shrimp
Prep Time: 20 minutes
Cook Time: 50 minutes
Serves 4

Nutritional Facts:

Calories-181
Total Fat-4g
Sat Fat-1g
Dietary Fiber-3g
Sugars-6g

Sodium- 238mg
Total Carbohydrates-16g
Trans Fat-0g
Protein-21g
Cholesterol-85mg

Stir-frying can be a not-so-good cook's rescue when entertaining. While the prep work takes some time, once it goes into the pan, it's easy and fun! This dish is low in saturated fat; it's a good source of protein, vitamin A, vitamin D, vitamin K, riboflavin, niacin, iron and a very good source of vitamin C and selenium.

Ingredients:

3 cups low sodium chicken stock
Pam olive oil spray
3 quarter sized slices of fresh ginger, lightly smashed
2 large garlic cloves, smashed
½ pound medium shrimp, shelled and cleaned
¼ lb shiitake mushrooms, thinly sliced
1 lb snow peas, thick stems discarded
1 tsp cornstarch
3 tbs rice wine
1 tsp asian sesame oil
Few drops of Tabasco sauce
2 large egg whites, lightly beaten

In medium saucepan, boil the chicken stock over high heat until reduced to 1 1/2 cups. About 20 minutes. Let cool. Heat a large wok or 5 quart saucepan. Add Pam spray and coat well. Add ginger and garlic and stir fry over high heat until deep golden, about 2-3 minutes. Remove and discard. Add shrimp to wok and cook over high heat, turning once, about 2-3 minutes. Using a slotted spoon, transfer shrimp to a bowl. Add shiitakes to wok and stir-fry for about 2 minutes. Add snow peas and stir fry for another 3 minutes. Transfer veggies to bowl. Stir the cornstarch into the chicken broth. Return wok to high heat and add stock mixture, rice wine, sesame oil and Tabasco. Stir until sauce thickens, about 5 minutes. Stir in shrimp. Add egg whites and cook without stirring until just beginning to set, about 10 seconds. Stir gently so the egg whites form shreds, then simmer for 30". Pour the shrimp and sauce over the pea shoots and shiitakes. Serve immediately.

Asian Style Foil Fish
Prep Time: 30 minutes
Cook Time: 20 minutes
Serves 4

Nutritional Facts:

Calories-370

Total Fat-18g

Sat Fat-3g

Dietary Fiber-3g

Sugars-2g

Sodium- 736mg

Total Carbohydrates-17g

Trans Fat-0g

Protein-36g

Cholesterol-101mg

This is a very flavorful dish. Unfortunately, any time you use soy sauce, even low sodium, you're going to end up with high sodium content. If you have high blood pressure you might want to watch that. Otherwise, just be prepared to be a little bloated the next day and enjoy the wonderful flavor! It's a good source of vitamin C, vitamin K, vitamin B6 and pantothenic acid. It's packed with protein and vitamin A.

Ingredients:

2 firm fish fillets or steaks, about 6 oz each

2 cups bok choy, chopped

¼ cup chopped shiitake mushrooms

2 scallions, chopped

Vegetable oil spray

1 tsp vegetable oil

1 tsp grated ginger root

1 or 2 garlic cloves, minced

2 tbs low sodium soy sauce

2 tsp dark sesame oil

1 tsp chili flakes

Preheat oven to 450. Take two 12 x 24" sheets of aluminum foil. Fold each sheet over to make a double thick square. Spray the center part of each square. Rinse fish. Layer the greens, mushrooms, fish, and scallions on the foil. In small bowl combine vegetable oil, grated ginger, garlic, soy sauce, sesame oil and chili flakes. Pour some of the sauce over fish in each packet. Fold the foil into airtight packets. Bake for 20 minutes. Open packets to make sure fish is cooked and transfer contents to plate.

Fun Food Tip: Potatoes will take food stains off your fingers. Just slice and rub raw potato on the stains and rinse your hands in water. NOW you know why you put that apple in there!

Charcoal-Broiled Shrimp
Prep Time: 40 minutes
Cook Time: 5 minutes
Serves 4

Nutritional Facts:

Calories-58

Total Fat-1g

Sat Fat-0g

Dietary Fiber-0g

Sugars-0g

Sodium- 64mg

Total Carbohydrates-2g

Trans Fat-0g

Protein-9g

Cholesterol-64mg

I love shrimp. It's quick, easy to prepare and picks up the flavor of whatever you're cooking it in fast. It's packed with protein, vitamin C, vitamin D, vitamin K, iron and selenium. If you're watching your cholesterol, make this crustacean a treat to have every so often.

Ingredients:

24 large shrimp. About 2 lbs, cleaned and deveined

1 tbs finely chopped fresh ginger

¼ tsp dried hot red pepper flakes

2 tbs finely chopped parsley

1 bay leaf

1 tsp chopped fresh thyme

Pam olive oil spray

Juice of ½ lemon

2 cloves garlic, crushed

Preheat a charcoal broiler. Lay the shrimp flat on a cookie sheet. Spray well with Pam. Combine the shrimp, ginger, pepper flakes, parsley, bay leaf, thyme, lemon juice and garlic in a mixing bowl. Let stand at room temperature for 30 minutes. Put the shrimp on the broiler and cook for about 5-6 minutes. Serve with vegetable of choice.

Fish Fillets in Foil
Prep Time: 25 minutes
Cook Time: 20 minutes
Serves 4

Nutritional Facts:

Calories-427

Total Fat-17g

Sat Fat-3g

Dietary Fiber-3g

Sugars-4g

Sodium- 153mg

Total Carbohydrates-10g

Trans Fat-0g

Protein-56g

Cholesterol-168mg

   This one dish meal is great and you can substitute any vegetables you like! (Personally, if you make this when I come over, please do NOT add brussel sprouts.) I also add fresh dill or basil when I have it. Have fun with this one. It's almost impossible to mess up. It's a good source of niacin, vitamin B6, vitamin B12, protein and vitamin C.

Ingredients:

2 ½ pounds boneless white fish like striped bass, flounder or fluke

Pam olive oil spray

1 cup thinly sliced onions

1 tsp finely minced garlic

1 ½ cored, seeded red pepper, cut into thin strips

2 cups thinly sliced Portobello mushroom caps

1 cup peeled, cubed red ripe tomatoes

1 bay leaf cut in half

¼ tsp dried thyme

1/8 tsp dried hot red pepper flakes

Fresh pepper to taste

   Pre-heat oven to 500 degrees. Cut fish into four pieces of equal size and weight. Cut 4 pieces of aluminum foil about 24" by 12". Spray large skillet with Pam. Heat over medium heat. Add onion, garlic, peppers and mushrooms. Cook until peppers and onions are wilted. Add the tomatoes, bay leaf and thyme. Add pepper flakes and pepper. Open up foil and spray with Pam. Place one fish fillet in center. Spoon about ¼ veggie mixture over the fillet. Fold foil over and seal the edges as securely as possible. Do the same for all pieces of fish. Arrange the fish packages on one or two baking sheets. Bake in the oven for 10 minutes. Serve by transferring fish to dinner plates.

Grilled Shrimp with Thai Lemongrass Marinade
Prep Time: 35 minutes plus 1 hour marinate time
Cook Time: 5 minutes
Serves 4

Nutritional Facts:

Calories-215
Total Fat-3g
Sat Fat-1g
Dietary Fiber-1g
Sugars-1g

Sodium- 974mg
Total Carbohydrates-10g
Trans Fat-0g
Protein-36g
Cholesterol-255mg

I know, I know…you're thinking "Holy crap! Look at the sodium in this one!" Well, relax. Most of this is from the marinade, and only a small portion stays on the shrimp. The rest you pour down the drain! There's lots of niacin, vitamin B12, iron, phosphorus and copper.

Ingredients:

3 garlic cloves, thinly sliced
3 Thai chilies, thinly sliced (use jalapeno if necessary)
2 stalks of fresh lemongrass, bottom third only, thinly sliced
1 shallot, sliced thin
1 tbs chopped fresh ginger
1/3 c low sodium soy sauce
¼ c splenda
¼ c fresh limejuice
¼ cup chopped cilantro
2 tsp ground coriander
Pepper
1 1/2 pounds large shrimp, cleaned and shelled

In a food processor, combine garlic, chilies, lemongrass, shallot and ginger, and process to a paste. Scrape into a bowl and stir in soy sauce, Splenda, limejuice, cilantro, coriander and pepper to taste. Take shrimp and mix into marinade. Let sit for one hour in refrigerator.

Light a grill. Thread shrimp on skewers and cook over a hot fire for about 2 minutes per side. Use leftover marinade to baste.

Light Shrimp Scampi
Prep Time: 20 minutes
Cook Time: 6 minutes
Serves 4

Nutritional Facts:

Calories-271

Total Fat-5g

Sat Fat-1g

Dietary Fiber-0g

Sugars-0g

Sodium- 409mg

Total Carbohydrates-6g

Trans Fat-0g

Protein-48g

Cholesterol-355mg

This is my very favorite shrimp scampi recipe EVER! Every time I serve it, people go nuts. Sometimes I'll whip up a batch, throw some toothpicks in the middle of the plate and use them as h'or doevres. Easy to make, easy to eat and no leftovers. I promise. Doesn't matter how much I make, if I don't hide some, it'll get eaten. If you're watching your carbs, just omit the breadcrumbs. It still has a lot of flavor. This recipe is a great source of protein, vitamin D and selenium.

Ingredients:

2 pounds of large shrimp

Pam olive oil spray

2 tsp finely chopped garlic

2 tablespoons finely chopped parsley

Few shakes of red pepper flakes, to taste

1 tsp dried oregano

1 tablespoon fresh breadcrumbs

Pepper to taste

Preheat broiler to high. Clean and split shrimp down the back. Rinse and pat dry. Place shrimp in one layer in lined baking dish. Spray with Pam. Put shrimp into large bowl, add all other ingredients and toss well. Replace shrimp in dish in one layer. Place shrimp under broiler about 3-4 inches from flame. Broil 5-6 minutes. No need to turn. Serve.

Poached Salmon with Cucumber Sauce
Prep Time: 15 minutes
Cook Time: 35 minutes
Serves 4

Nutritional Facts:

Calories-388

Total Fat-15g

Sat Fat-2g

Dietary Fiber-1g

Sugars-3g

Sodium- 533mg

Total Carbohydrates-15g

Trans Fat-0g

Protein-47g

Cholesterol-116mg

This is a great summer dish. You can serve the salmon hot or cold and the sauce can be refrigerated for up to a week ahead. The sodium level can be decreased by using low sodium fish or chicken stock. It's a good source of riboflavin, pantothenic acid, protein, vitamin B6, vitamin B12 and niacin.

Ingredients:
2 Tbs white wine vinegar
4 cups fish stock
4 salmon steaks
Sauce:
2 large cucumbers, seeded and peeled
1/3 bunch dill (3 tbs) finely chopped
1 cup fat free sour cream or yogurt
Pepper
Lemon juice

For the Sauce:
Coarsely chop cucumbers. Put in processor on pulse. Scraping sides of bowl, process until it looks like a slurpy. Strain it well, getting as much liquid out as possible without it getting too dry. Add dill, sour cream, pepper and touch of lemon juice. Set sauce aside.

For the Fish:
Put white wine vinegar in a pan and cover. Reduce until just a bit left. Add fish stock. Bring to a boil. Turn off flame. Immediately put in salmon steaks. Cover. Check after about 5 minutes. If not done yet, relight flame and heat until just before boiling. Turn off again. Place salmon on plate and top with sauce.

Poached Trout
Prep Time: 20 minutes
Cook Time: 35 minutes
Serves 4

Nutritional Facts:

Calories-153

Total Fat-7g

Sat Fat-2g

Dietary Fiber-0g

Sugars-0g

Sodium- 66mg

Total Carbohydrates-2g

Trans Fat-0g

Protein-8g

Cholesterol-23mg

This is a nice healthy dish. You can use another white fish instead and it will be just as good. It's low sodium, a good source of protein, vitamin K and a very good source of vitamin B12.

Ingredients:

3 cups of water

1 cup dry white wine

2 tbs fresh chives, chopped

2 tbs minced basil leaves

1 tbs chopped fresh dill

1 tbs chopped rosemary

Fresh pepper to taste

1 strip of lemon zest, about 2" long

2 fresh brook trout, cleaned and deboned

3 tbs smart balance butter spread, melted

In a large pot, place water, wine, herbs, spices and lemon zest. Bring to a boil. Lower heat and simmer for 10 minutes. Gently place trout in liquid. Simmer until firm to the touch, about 10 minutes. Using 2 spatulas, lift the trout out and place on a dinner plate. Mix the melted Smart Balance with 2 tbs cooking liquid. Spoon over fish and serve.

Shrimp in New Orleans Sauce

Prep Time: 30 minutes
Cook Time: 23 minutes
Serves 4

Nutritional Facts:

Calories-238
Total Fat-8g
Sat Fat-2g
Dietary Fiber-5g
Sugars-6g

Sodium- 306mg
Total Carbohydrates-21g
Trans Fat-0g
Protein-33g
Cholesterol-226mg

I like to use extra garlic for this recipe…but then again, I use extra garlic for most recipes. I also love spicy food, so this is a win-win for me. It has lots of vitamin D, vitamin B6, Protein, vitamin A, vitamin C, vitamin K and selenium.

Ingredients:

1 ¼ pounds raw shrimp in shell
4 tablespoons Smart Balance margarine
2 cups finely chopped onion
2 teaspoons minced garlic
1 cup chopped celery
2 cups red and green pepper, cored, seeded and cut into 1" pieces.
Pepper to taste
3 cups fresh tomatoes cut into small cubes
¼ cup finely chopped fresh parsley
1 bay leaf
Tabasco Sauce to taste

Peel and clean shrimp. Heat 2 tablespoons Smart Balance in a saucepan and add onion and garlic. Cook on medium/low heat about 5 minutes. Add celery and peppers. Add pepper to taste. Cook around 4 minutes, stirring often. Add tomatoes, parsley and bay leaf. Cover. At the boil, cook about 10 minutes. Add Tabasco. In separate skillet, heat remaining Smart Balance and the shrimp. Sprinkle with pepper. Stir. Cook about one minute. Spoon tomato mixture over shrimp and stir. Bring to a boil. Serve.

South of the Border Shrimp
Prep Time: 25 minutes
Cook Time: 14 minutes
Serves 4

Nutritional Facts:

Calories-264

Total Fat-9g

Sat Fat-2g

Dietary Fiber-2g

Sugars-3g

Sodium- 311mg

Total Carbohydrates-11g

Trans Fat-0g

Protein-35g

Cholesterol-255mg

   Another spicy dish, this time with a Mexican flavor. It has vitamin B12 and phosphorus and is a very good source of protein, vitamin D and selenium.

Ingredients:

Olive oil cooking spray

1 ½ cups chopped white onion

1 tsp ground cumin

2 tsp chili powder

1 ½ pounds medium shrimp peeled and deveined

3 garlic cloves, minced

2 Tbs Smart Balance butter substitute

2 shakes hot pepper sauce, or to taste

¼ cup fresh limejuice

¼ cup finely chopped green onions

   Spray large non-stick skillet with cooking spray. Heat over medium high flame. Add onion and sauté about 3 minutes. Add cumin, chili powder, shrimp and garlic. Sauté about 4 minutes. Remove from heat. Add Smart Balance and hot sauce. Stir in lime juice and green onions. Serves 4.

Turkey for Pocket Sandwiches
Prep Time: 15 minutes
Cook Time: 25 minutes
Serves 4

Nutritional Facts:

Calories-250

Total Fat-7g

Sat Fat-2g

Dietary Fiber-2g

Sugars-0g

Sodium- 166mg

Total Carbohydrates-9g

Trans Fat-0g

Protein-31g

Cholesterol-134mg

This is one of my Mom's recipes. She used to make this for me for lunches and light dinners. It was always one I relied on after leaving home. There's vitamin A, niacin, vitamin B6 and selenium. Lots of protein and vitamin C, too!

Ingredients:

1 ½ lbs ground turkey

1 large onion, chopped

2 large cloves garlic, minced

2 large red or yellow peppers, chopped

1 tbs fresh oregano leaves or 1 tsp dry

1 tbs fresh thyme or 1 tsp dry

Black pepper to taste

5 tbs red wine vinegar

Heat nonstick skillet over medium heat. Add turkey, breaking it up as you stir until meat begins to brown. Add onions, garlic, red and yellow peppers, oregano, thyme and pepper. Cook over medium heat until onion softens. Add vinegar and cook quickly to reduce liquid, about 2 minutes. Adjust seasonings. Serve with pita pockets or lettuce for wraps.

Oven Roasted Vegetables with Italian-Style Turkey Sausage
Prep Time: 15 minutes
Cook Time: 40 minutes
Serves 4

Nutritional Facts:

Calories-403

Total Fat-8g

Sat Fat-2g

Dietary Fiber-25g

Sugars-8g

Sodium- 363mg

Total Carbohydrates-60g

Trans Fat-0g

Protein-29g

Cholesterol-44mg

Another one of my favorite recipes, it can be a bit of a challenge to find a healthy turkey or chicken sausage without nitrates, nitrites, etc. (Try Whole Foods) The carbohydrates are seemingly high, but they're from fibrous sources, not starch…an important distinction. Again, like other recipes with a lot of different vegetables, be creative and add what you like! There's a lot of protein, vitamin C, vitamin B6, folate, magnesium, phosphorus, potassium, fiber and manganese.

Ingredients:

2 medium eggplants, trimmed
3 medium zucchini, trimmed
Pam olive oil spray
6 garlic cloves
8 Italian-flavored turkey (or chicken) sausages
4 plum tomatoes
2 11 oz cans of canellini beans
Fresh pepper to taste
1 bunch fresh basil, torn into coarse pieces
Soy Parmesan cheese

Preheat oven to 400 degrees. Cut eggplant and zucchini into bite-sized chunks. Spray Pam into large roasting pan. Heat in preheated oven for 3 minutes. Add eggplant, zucchini and garlic. Stir until coated with Pam. Cook in oven for 10 minutes. Remove roasting pan and stir. Lightly prick sausages and add to roasting pan. Return pan to oven. Roast for 20 more minutes or so, turning once during cooking, until sausages are golden brown.

Meanwhile, coarsely chop the plum tomatoes and drain the beans. Remove the sausages from the oven and stir in the tomatoes and beans. Season to taste with pepper, then return to oven for 5 minutes or so. Sprinkle with torn basil and soy cheese. Serve immediately.

Quick Italian Chili-1 Skillet Meal
Prep Time: 20 minutes
Cook Time: 40 minutes
Serves 4

Nutritional Facts:
Calories-342

Total Fat-17g

Sat Fat- 4g

Dietary Fiber-4g

Sugars-11g

Sodium- 169mg

Total Carbohydrates-19g

Trans Fat-0g

Protein-29g

Cholesterol-119mg

This recipe is perfect for those nights where you've worked late or the kids have practice and not a lot of time. It's low in sodium, a good source of vitamin K, niacin, vitamin B6 and selenium.

Ingredients:
Olive oil spray

6oz mushrooms, preferably Portobello, chopped small

1 large red pepper, chopped small

1 large onion, chopped small

4 cloves of garlic, minced

2 lbs ground turkey

1 Tbsp dried basil

½ tsp dried red pepper flakes

½ tsp fennel seeds

1 Tbsp dried oregano

1 jar (16oz) low sodium spaghetti sauce or homemade sauce (see recipe)

Spray inside of a 4 qt. Saucepan with oil to cover and brown turkey over medium flame. Pour off excess fat and transfer to bowl. In the same pan, re-spray with oil and over medium heat, cook garlic and onion for 4 minutes or until onion starts to turn translucent. Add red pepper and cook another 3 minutes. Add mushrooms and all spices and cook, stirring occasionally for 5 minutes. Return turkey meat to pan.   Stir for one minute. Add spaghetti sauce. Lower heat a bit, cover and cook to bubbling. About 3 minutes. Serve alone in bowls with parmesan or soy parmesan, over spaghetti squash or layer with thinly sliced, baked eggplant for "lasagna."

"The trouble with eating Italian food is that 5 or 6 days later you're hungry again."
George Miller, British writer

Turkey Chili
Prep Time: 15 minutes
Cook Time: 55 minutes
Serves 4

Nutritional Facts:

Calories-473

Total Fat-16g

Sat Fat-4g

Dietary Fiber-14g

Sugars-12g

Sodium- 157mg

Total Carbohydrates-43g

Trans Fat-0g

Protein-43g

Cholesterol-134mg

I love chili. Any kind, which is why there are a few variations in the book. It's nutritious, easy and one-dish. If you're really watching carbohydrates, omit the beans, although they're a great source of fiber. As is, this recipe has vitamin B6, iron, phosphorus and selenium and is a great source of protein and vitamin C.

Ingredients:

1 14oz. can of stewed tomatoes, low sodium

1 28 oz. can of whole tomatoes, low sodium

1 regular onion, chopped small

1 red or green pepper sliced very thin

2 tbs. chili sauce

1 tsp chili powder

1 tsp cumin

2 Tbs fresh cilantro, chopped

3 cloves of garlic, chopped

½ tsp. onion powder

1 14oz can of kidney beans

1-1 ½ pounds ground turkey

Tabasco sauce to taste

Olive oil spray

Spray large, deep pan with Pam. On medium-high heat, brown ground turkey until almost cooked. Take out meat, drain and place in a bowl on the side. Re-spray pan and over medium heat, add garlic, stir and cook for 1 minute. Add onion and red pepper and cook until onion starts to wilt and turn translucent. Add all tomatoes. Stir and cook 3 minutes. Add all other ingredients and simmer for 8 minutes. Return meat and simmer for another 25 minutes. Serve.

Basic Sauté of Chicken with Herbs
Prep Time: 15 minutes
Cook Time: 20 minutes
Serves 4

Nutritional Facts:

Calories-57

Total Fat-4g

Sat Fat- 0g

Dietary Fiber-2g

Sugars-1g

Sodium- 33mg

Total Carbohydrates-2g

Trans Fat-0g

Protein-9g

Cholesterol-21mg

This is one of the recipes that I made after I moved out of my parent's house, way back when. I think I got the original from the New York Times. I've changed it to make it healthier…of course. I love that it still stands as the basic start to my creative endeavors. It has a lot of protein and niacin, as well as vitamin B6, phosphorus and selenium.

Ingredients:

2 pounds of chicken breasts, about 4 halves.

Freshly ground pepper

Pam olive oil spray

1 tsp finely chopped fresh rosemary, thyme or sage (or a mix)

1 tbs finely chopped shallots

3 tbs dry white wine

½ cup low sodium chicken broth

Sprinkle chicken with pepper. Spray 4 or 5 quart sauté pan with Pam. Heat over medium/high flame. Add chicken in one layer. Cook about 5 minutes on one side. Turn over. Add herbs. Cook about 5 minutes longer or until just cooked through. Remove chicken and arrange on serving dish. Keep warm. Add shallots to pan and stir for one minute. Add wine and continue to cook for 4 minutes, stirring occasionally. Add chicken broth and simmer, stirring well to blend. Pour over chicken and serve.

Chicken Breasts With Peppers
Prep Time: 15 minutes
Cook Time: 15 minutes
Serves 4

Nutritional Facts:

Calories-94

Total Fat-1g

Sat Fat-1g

Dietary Fiber-2g

Sugars-2g

Sodium- 26mg

Total Carbohydrates-5g

Trans Fat-0g

Protein-9g

Cholesterol-21mg

As you can see, this is another version of the basic recipe of chicken. I just added some veggies. Fun stuff, this cooking, huh? This is a good source of protein, vitamin A, vitamin C, vitamin K, niacin and vitamin B6.

Ingredients:
2 whole boneless chicken breasts, about 2 pounds, cut in half

Pepper to taste

Pam cooking spray

1 tsp minced garlic

½ pound red or green pepper, cored, seeded and cut into thin strips

½ cup dry white wine

1 tbs fresh chopped parsley

Sprinkle chicken with pepper. Spray large skillet with Pam. Heat over medium-high heat. Add chicken pieces. Cook about 3 minutes or until golden brown. Turn and cook another 3 minutes. Add garlic and pepper strips. Cook about 4 minutes. Add wine and cover. Cook another 3 minutes or so. Take chicken out and place on a serving plate. Pour peppers over chicken and sprinkle with parsley.

Baked Chicken and Wild Rice
Prep Time: 15 minutes
Cook Time: 40 minutes
Serves 4

Nutritional Facts:

Calories-245

Total Fat-2g

Sat Fat-0g

Dietary Fiber-4g

Sugars-5g

Sodium- 60 mg

Total Carbohydrates-43g

Trans Fat-0g

Protein-16g

Cholesterol-21mg

This is a combination of my Mother's chicken and rice dish with healthier alternatives. She started with a rice mix, which had sugar included in the ingredients...not to mention some additives I can't pronounce. But, when I was a kid, who knew from these things? I've substituted brown and wild rice and the citrus adds a great taste mixed with the spices! It's a hearty one-dish meal. It's low in sodium and saturated fat, a great source of protein, niacin, vitamin B6, vitamin C, vitamin K and manganese.

Ingredients:
½ cup wild rice
½ cup brown rice
1 14.5 oz can low sodium tomatoes, chopped, with juice.
1/4 cup fresh orange juice
¼ cup fresh limejuice
1 cup low-sodium, fat free chicken broth
1/2 cup Italian parsley, chopped
½ cup fresh cilantro, chopped
1 medium onion, sliced thin
3 cloves of garlic, sliced thin or minced
½ tsp cumin
½ tsp pepper
¼ tsp red pepper flakes
½ tsp chili powder
4 boneless, skinless chicken breasts (about 2 pounds)

Heat oven to 400. In a large bowl, mix the rice, tomatoes and juice, lime and orange juice, parsley, cilantro, onion, garlic, cumin, ¼ tsp of pepper, chili powder and red pepper flakes. Transfer to a 9 x 13" baking dish. Rinse the chicken and pat dry. Season with the rest of the pepper. Place chicken ion the rice. Cover dish with foil and bake until the chicken is cooked, about 35-40 minutes. Remove and let stand for about 5 minutes. Serve.

Ratatouille with Chicken Sausage
Prep time: 15 minutes
Cook time: 30 minutes
Serves 4

Nutritional Facts:

Calories-98

Total Fat-1g

Sat Fat-1g

Dietary Fiber-6g

Sugars-6g

Sodium-28 mg

Total Carbohydrates-17g

Trans Fat-0g

Protein-7g

Cholesterol-10mg

As I said in the Oven Roasted Veggies with Turkey Sausage recipe, I find great, healthy sausages at Whole Foods Market. There are vegan sausages that work well here, too. A great winter dish. It's low in saturated fat and sodium, has lots of folate, iron, magnesium, phosphorus, potassium, and copper. The fiber is high, as well as the vitamin A, vitamin C, vitamin K, vitamin B6 and manganese. All without a high calorie count. Don't you love when that happens?

Ingredients:

Olive oil spray

1 medium onion, chopped

1 small eggplant, unpeeled, cut into small chunks

1 red bell pepper cut into ½" pieces

1 yellow pepper, cut into ½" pieces

3 cloves garlic, thinly sliced

1 14.5oz can of low sodium diced or stewed tomatoes, undrained

½ tsp black pepper

¼ tsp red pepper flakes

4 no-nitrite chicken breast sausages, about 1 ½-2 lbs

½ cup fresh flat leaf parsley, finely chopped

Heat oven to 400. Spray oil in large skillet over med-high heat. Add onion and cook for about 2 minutes. Add eggplant and bell peppers and cook 3 more minutes. Add garlic, tomatoes and juice, pepper, red pepper and ¼ cup water. Bring to a boil. Put the sausages in the skillet, in one layer, pushed into the vegetables. Spoon more veggies over them. Transfer skillet to oven and cook, uncovered for about 30 minutes. Stir in the chopped parsley. Serve.

Oriental Grilled Chicken

Prep Time: 15 minutes
Marinating Time: 6 hours
Cook Time: 30-40 minutes
Serves 4

Nutritional Facts:

Calories-280
Total Fat-12g
Sat Fat-2g
Dietary Fiber-2g
Sugars-0g

Sodium- 20 mg
Total Carbohydrates-4g
Trans Fat-0g
Protein-38g
Cholesterol-121mg

This recipe works best when you start it in the morning (it doesn't take long to throw everything together) and let it marinate in the 'fridge until dinner. It's low in sodium, a good source of vitamin B6, phosphorus and selenium. Lots of protein and niacin!

Ingredients:
¼ cup toasted sesame seeds
¼ cup minced fresh ginger
2 tbs sesame oil
2 tbs rice vinegar
1 tsp dried red pepper flakes
1 tsp Chinese 5 spice powder
1 chicken, about 3-4 pounds, cleaned and quartered.

In a very large bowl, stir in all ingredients but the chicken. Add the quartered bird, making sure all parts are covered with marinade. Cover bowl with plastic wrap and refrigerate for about 6 hours. Heat up grill. Grill chicken over medium heat, turning occasionally, for about 30 minutes.

Chicken in Red Wine Sauce
Prep Time: 12 minutes
Cook Time: 20 minutes
Serves 4

Nutritional Facts:

Calories-272

Total Fat-3g

Sat Fat-1g

Dietary Fiber-1g

Sugars-1g

Sodium- 130 mg

Total Carbohydrates-6g

Trans Fat-0g

Protein-43g

Cholesterol-103mg

I love cooking with a skillet. You don't have to wait until the oven or grill is heated, it's basically one dish and things cook very quickly. You can serve this dish for company. It's that nice. It's a good source of vitamin B6, phosphorus, and selenium, and has lots of protein, vitamin K and niacin.

Ingredients:
3 boneless chicken breasts (6 halves) cut into large pieces.
Pepper
Butter flavored cooking spray
¼ pound exotic mushrooms, sliced
¼ cup chopped shallots
2 cloves garlic, finely chopped
1 cup dry red wine
½ cup low sodium chicken broth
1 bay leaf
¼ c chopped parsley
½ tsp dried thyme

Sprinkle chicken with pepper. Spray large skillet with cooking spray and add chicken in one layer. Cook chicken over medium heat about 3 minutes. Turn and cook 3 minutes more. Add mushrooms, shallots and garlic and stir to blend. Cook about 2 minutes, then add wine and broth and bring to low boil. Add all herbs and lower heat. Cook another 6-8 minutes, covered.

Chicken Pesto

Prep Time: 10 minutes
Cook Time: 20 minutes
Serves 4

Nutritional Facts:

Calories-144
Total Fat-2g
Sat Fat-0g
Dietary Fiber-0g
Sugars-0g

Sodium- 105 mg
Total Carbohydrates-1g
Trans Fat-0g
Protein-29g
Cholesterol-68mg

This is a really quick and easy one. Although this recipe calls for dried herbs, use fresh basil when you can. Use about 2 tbs to substitute and puree in the blender with the rest of the ingredients. This is low in saturated fats and a good source of vitamin K and phosphorus. It's all protein and has lots of niacin, vitamin B6 and selenium.

Ingredients:

4 chicken breasts, skinned
2 oz. egg whites
1 tsp. parsley
½ tsp basil
½ tsp. oregano
½ tsp. thyme
Dash of pepper
2 cloves of garlic

Place egg whites, parsley, basil, oregano, thyme, pepper and garlic in blender. Puree until they form a smooth paste. Coat chicken with pesto mixture and place on a sheet pan coated with Pam. Bake at 350 for 15-20 minutes.

Chicken with Peppers
Prep Time: 15 minutes
Cook Time: 25 minutes
Serves 4

Nutritional Facts:

Calories-177

Total Fat-2g

Sat Fat: 1g

Dietary Fiber-2g

Sugars-4g

Sodium- 87 mg

Total Carbohydrates-9g

Trans Fat-0g

Protein-29g

Cholesterol-68mg

This is one of my go-to recipes when I'm cooking for myself. Personally, I like it with red and yellow peppers, plus I add another garlic clove. That's the beauty of cooking. It's an "art." Some people like to work with watercolors, some like finger painting. Have fun with it and make it your own. This recipe has high protein, vitamin C, niacin and vitamin B6 along with some vitamin A, phosphorus and the ever-popular selenium.

Ingredients:

Pam olive oil spray

1 large sweet onion, sliced

2 cloves of garlic, chopped

1 green and 1 red pepper, sliced

1 tsp dried oregano

1 tbs balsamic vinegar

Fresh pepper to taste

4 chicken breasts, skinless and boneless, quartered

¼ cup low sodium chicken broth

Spray Pam well into 3-qt. sauté pan. Add onion and garlic and sauté slowly over medium-low heat until translucent. About 5 minutes. Add peppers, oregano, balsamic vinegar and pepper to taste. Add broth. Raise heat to medium high and sauté while stirring for 3 minutes. Transfer to bowl. Re-spray Pam in pan and heat for 2 minutes. Add chicken breasts. Turn about every 30 seconds until slightly brown on both sides. Return pepper mixture to pan. Cover and cook over medium heat for 5 minutes.

Tequila Marinated Beef for Fajitas
(Can also use Chicken)
Prep Time: 10 minutes plus one day marinate time
Cook Time: 25 minutes
Serves 4

Nutritional Facts:

Calories-330

Total Fat-14g

Sat Fat-0g

Dietary Fiber-1g

Sugars-1g

Sodium- 116 mg

Total Carbohydrates46g

Trans Fat-0g

Protein-36g

Cholesterol-97mg

The above nutritional facts are for using beef. Chicken would be a bit less fat and cholesterol. Skirt steak marinates well, however, and I like it better here. These fajitas are a real crowd pleaser. Try this for a Superbowl party. It's a good source of vitamin B6, phosphorus, zinc and selenium and a very good source of protein and vitamin B12.

Ingredients:

3 lb skirt steak

½ cup fresh limejuice

Olive oil spray

1/2 cup tequila

1 tsp ground cumin

1 tsp dried oregano

½ tsp fresh ground pepper

5 large cloves of garlic

6 small onions cut in half

Trim excess fat from the meat and cut the meat crosswise into long strips about ½" wide. Place the strips in a shallow, non-reactive dish. Spray meat with olive oil spray. In a bowl, stir together the lime juice, tequila, cumin, oregano, pepper and garlic. Pour over the meat, coating well. Cover with plastic wrap and refrigerate for 24 hours, turning occasionally. In a heavy frying pan coated with olive oil spray, add the onion halves and cook over medium heat until well browned, about 6-8minutes. Stir constantly. Transfer to plate. Re-spray pan. Turn heat up to high. Drain the meat and reserve the marinade.   Add meat to pan and cook turning once and basting with the marinade about 2 minutes each side for medium-rare. Transfer to plate and serve with onions.

Fun Food Tip: Honey is a home remedy for skin blemishes. Cover the blemish with a dab of honey. Place a Band-Aid over it. It kills the bacteria, keeps the skin sterile and speeds healing. It works overnight. You'll just need to change your pillowcase in the morning.

Ground Beef with Lebanese Spices
Prep Time: 10 minutes
Cook Time: Varies
Serves 4

Nutritional Facts:

Calories-275

Total Fat-15g

Sat Fat-4g

Dietary Fiber-1g

Sugars-1g

Sodium- 123 mg

Total Carbohydrates-4g

Trans Fat-0g

Protein-31g

Cholesterol-112mg

Again, the nutritional breakdown is for basic ground beef. The fat and cholesterol levels go down for extra lean or turkey. I like to double or triple this recipe and freeze what I don't use. It makes a nice change from Italian spices when you're making a red sauce. It's low in sodium and is a very good source of protein, vitamin K and selenium.

Ingredients:

2 lbs lean ground beef or ground turkey

1 cup grated onion

½ cup finely minced flat leaf parsley

½ tsp fresh ground pepper

2 tsp cumin

1 tsp cinnamon

½ tsp allspice

In a bowl ,combine all ingredients. Knead with your hands. Cover and chill for 1 hour. Use for hamburgers, meatloaf or in a sauce.

Grilled Salmon and White Bean Salad
Prep Time: (Grilling-about 8 minutes, Parboiling green beans about 10) 15 minutes
Cook Time: 2 hours 10 minutes
Serves 4

Nutritional Facts:

Calories-331

Total Fat-13g

Sat Fat-2g

Dietary Fiber-11g

Sugars-1g

Sodium- 45 mg

Total Carbohydrates-29g

Trans Fat-0g

Protein-26g

Cholesterol-46mg

The fat grams may seem high here, but you need olive oil to make this taste just right. It's a healthy fat so don't worry about it. You can use leftover salmon or tuna to make this, as well. There are lots of fiber in this as well as niacin, vitamin B6, folate, vitamin B12, phosphorus and selenium.

Ingredients:

1 1/2 cup skinless grilled salmon pieces

2 cup cooked white beans,

1 cup cooked green beans

2 tablespoon extra virgin olive oil

2 tablespoon fresh lemon juice

1 teaspoon finely grated lemon zest

Freshly ground pepper

1 cup grape tomatoes,

1/3 cup thinly sliced red onion,

1 1/2 teaspoon thinly shredded fresh sage or minced rosemary leaves

Whisk together oil, lemon juice and zest, and pepper. Toss salmon with 1 tablespoon dressing. Toss white and green beans, tomatoes, onion, and sage in bowl with remaining dressing. Divide among 4 plates; top with salmon. Serve at once, or chill in refrigerator up to 2 hours

Herb-Marinated Lamb Chops
Prep Time: 50 minutes (plus overnight)
Cook Time: 25 minutes
Serves 4

Nutritional Facts:

Calories-233

Total Fat-8g

Sat Fat-2g

Dietary Fiber-1g

Sugars-0g

Sodium- 182 mg

Total Carbohydrates-3g

Trans Fat-0g

Protein-36g

Cholesterol-112mg

These lamb chops are outrageous on a grill. They taste great in an oven, but give 'em a shot outdoors and you'll be hooked. Add some asparagus and you've got a great, low carb meal. This recipe is high in protein, niacin, vitamin B12 and zinc.

Ingredients:

8 sprigs thyme

8 large sprigs rosemary

8 large clove garlic,

3 tablespoon extra-virgin olive oil

2 teaspoon crushed peppercorns

8 double-cut rib lamb chops

Crush thyme and rosemary sprigs with the flat side of a knife; place in a large glass baking dish with the garlic, olive oil, and peppercorns. Add the lamb chops and toss to coat. Cover with plastic and refrigerate at least 1½ hours or overnight. Remove chops from refrigerator half an hour before cooking. Preheat oven to 400°F. Scrape off marinade. Heat a 12-inch ovenproof skillet over medium-high heat. Sear chops on both sides, about 3 minutes each. (Cook in batches, transferring chops to a warm plate.) Arrange chops in skillet on their edges, fat side down, with bones facing up. Transfer skillet to oven and roast 5 to 8 minutes until medium-rare and a meat thermometer registers about 130°F. Transfer chops to cutting board; cover loosely with foil. Let rest 8 minutes. Slice chops between the bones.

Marinated Skirt Steak
Prep Time: 1 hour, 10 minutes
Cook Time: 10 minutes
Serves 4

Nutritional Facts:

Calories-352

Total Fat-21g

Sat Fat: 6g

Dietary Fiber-0g

Sugars-1g

Sodium- 159 mg

Total Carbohydrates-3g

Trans Fat-0g

Protein-36g

Cholesterol-97mg

Skirt steak is one of the better meats to marinade as it picks up the flavor so easily and the well-marbled cut keeps moist. This interesting combination of mustard, cilantro and garlic explodes with flavor; so simple side dishes go best with it. It's a good source of vitamin B6, zinc and selenium.

Ingredients:

1 1/2 pounds skirt steak

1 tbs dijon mustard

1/4 cup chopped cilantro

Grated zest of 1/2 lemon

2 tbs balsamic vinegar

2 tbs olive oil

1/2 tsp black pepper

2 roasted garlic cloves

To make the marinade, mix the Dijon mustard with chopped cilantro, lemon zest, balsamic vinegar, 2 tbsp. Olive oil, and black pepper. Soak the steak in the marinade for one hour in a covered container.

Use a broiler and cook the steak, with garlic cloves, for 5 minutes on each side, with broiler set to high. Or, sauté the steak in a heavy pan with 2 cloves of garlic.

As an alternate, you can sear in a grill pan on top of stove over high heat and then place in a 450° F oven for 10 to 15 minutes, to desired doneness (130 degrees with instant read thermometer would equal medium rare.)

Italian-Style Beef Burgers
Prep Time: 15 minutes
Cook Time: 8-10 minutes
Serves 4

Nutritional Facts:

Calories-341

Total Fat-24g

Sat Fat-9g

Dietary Fiber-0g

Sugars-0g

Sodium- 95 mg

Total Carbohydrates-2g

Trans Fat-0g

Protein-28g

Cholesterol-97mg

I splurged when making this recipe and used ground chuck, which is a little higher in fat. Adding the pine nuts adds to the higher fat content. You can leave them out, but the flavor suffers. Just enjoy these for what they are. If you are little more fat conscious than most, just substitute ground turkey or chicken and the fat grams head way down. Adkins enthusiasts enjoy as is!! It's all protein with lots of vitamin B12 and zinc!

Ingredients:
1 1/2 pound extra-lean ground beef chuck
2 tablespoon grated soy Parmesan cheese
2 tablespoons pine nuts, toasted, if preferred
1 teaspoon dried basil
1 teaspoon dried oregano
3/4 teaspoon minced fresh garlic
1/4 teaspoon ground black pepper

Place the broiler rack 2" to 3" from the heat source and preheat the broiler. Place the beef in a large bowl and break into pieces. Add the soy cheese, nuts, basil, oregano, garlic, and pepper. Using a fork, gently combine the beef and seasonings. Divide the meat into 4 even pieces and gently form into burgers approximately 4" in diameter and 1" thick. Place on a broiling pan, and cook until the top is browned, 4 to 6 minutes. Turn, and cook until done and a meat thermometer registers 160°F for medium, 4 to 6 minutes.

Pork Fajitas with Pan Roasted Peppers

Prep Time: 30 minutes
Cook Time: 15 minutes
Serves 4

Nutritional Facts:

Calories-223

Total Fat-9g

Sat Fat-3g

Dietary Fiber-2g

Sugars-5g

Sodium- 57 mg

Total Carbohydrates-9g

Trans Fat-0g

Protein-26g

Cholesterol-62mg

To be perfectly honest, I don't really cook with pork. Not because I don't like it, but because I grew up in a kosher home, so pork wasn't an option. I had help with this one when one of my friends said, "You have to put pork recipes in there! Other people DO eat it, ya know!" So I did. Who knew pork could be lean? Wow. Learn somethin' new every day. Use low carb tortillas and you'll be filled to the max with these easy, delicious fajitas. They have riboflavin, niacin, vitamin B6 and phosphorus. This has a lot of vitamin A, vitamin C, thiamine and selenium.

Ingredients:

1 1/4 pound boneless pork loin chops,

Zest and juice of 1 lime

3 cloves garlic,

1/4 teaspoon cayenne pepper

1/4 teaspoon ground black pepper

2 teaspoons plus cooking spray made with canola oil

3 large bell peppers (mixed colors), sliced

1 extra large onion, sliced

1 to 2 jalapeno peppers, chopped

1 cup loosely packed cilantro leaves,

12 6-inch low carb flour tortillas, (optional)

Slice pork into long, 1/2 inch-thick strips. Place in a bowl with zest, half the lime juice, garlic, cayenne, black pepper, and 2 teaspoons oil; toss to coat. Marinate at room temperature 20 minutes (or longer, or overnight, in the fridge).

Spray oil in a wok (or 12-inch nonstick skillet) over medium-high heat. Add bell peppers, onion, and jalapeno stir-fry until onions and peppers are soft and slightly charred, 6 to 8 minutes. Transfer to a metal bowl and toss with cilantro and remaining limejuice; cover with foil and keep warm.

Return wok to medium-high heat. Spray pan again and add the pork; stir-fry until meat is seared and just cooked through, 3 to 4 minutes. Place pork in warmed tortillas and top with vegetables.

Spicy Tofu Stew
Prep Time: 10 minutes
Cook Time: 20 minutes
Serves 4

Nutritional Facts:

Calories-324

Total Fat-12g

Sat Fat-4g

Dietary Fiber-4g

Sugars-3g

Sodium- 203 mg

Total Carbohydrates-10g

Trans Fat-0g

Protein-35g

Cholesterol-0mg

I love stir-frying. I have an old Calphelon wok that's practically see-through; I've used it so much. This vegan dish is full of flavor and spice. It has a good amount of protein, phosphorus, copper and selenium with a high amount of calcium and manganese.

Ingredients:
Vegetable oil spray
1 large clove garlic
1 1/2 ounce fresh ginger
2 (or more) fresh red Thai chilies
4 15-oz. firm or extra-firm tofu cakes, cubed
1 tablespoon Chinese reduced sodium soy sauce
1 tablespoon Chinese white rice vinegar
1 teaspoon sesame oil
1 scallion, sliced thin, white only

Heat oil in a heavy-bottom pan or wok over medium heat. Stir-fry garlic, ginger, and chiles until fragrant and lightly golden, about 3 minutes. Add tofu, soy sauce, vinegar, and sesame oil. Reduce heat to low, cover pan, and braise for 15 minutes. Garnish with scallion.

Vegetarian Chili
Prep Time: 15 minutes
Cook Time: 45 minutes
Serves 4

Nutritional Facts:

Calories: 133
Total Fat: 6g
Sat Fat: 1g
Dietary Fiber-5g
Sugars-6g

Sodium- 55 mg
Total Carbohydrates-13g
Trans Fat-0g
Protein-11g
Cholesterol-0mg

I know, I know. Another chili recipe. I can't help it. I used to live in Colorado and it was cold. Really, really, really cold for 9 months a year. I needed recipes to warm my insides as well as a hot bath warmed my outside. This vegan version has a load of vitamins and minerals in it like vitamin B6, folate, iron, magnesium, phosphorus, potassium, copper and selenium. And who could forget fiber, protein, vitamin A, vitamin C, vitamin K, calcium and manganese? Who needs daily vitamins when you make this?

Ingredients:
Canola oil spray
1 cup scallions, sliced
2 - garlic cloves
16 ounces firm tofu, cubed
1 tablespoon chili powder
1/4 teaspoon ground red pepper
1 14 1/2-oz can stewed tomatoes
2 tablespoon red wine vinegar
1 1/4 cups canned black beans
1 tablespoon cilantro
1 cup sweet red peppers, diced

Warm the oil in a 2-quart saucepan over medium heat. Add the scallions, sweet red peppers and garlic, sautéing for 4 to 5 minutes. Crumble the tofu and add to the pan. Stir frequently for 5 to 7 minutes. Add the chili powder and ground red pepper. Stir frequently for 2 minutes. Add the tomatoes and red wine vinegar. Bring to a boil. Reduce the heat and simmer for 20 to 30 minutes. Stir in the black beans and cilantro. Simmer for 5 minutes.

Lean Meatballs

Prep Time: 15 minutes
Cook Time: 25 minutes
Serves 6

Nutritional Facts:

Calories-190

Total Fat-7g

Sat Fat-3g

Dietary Fiber-1g

Sugars-1g

Sodium--134mg

Total Carbohydrates-4g

Trans Fat-2g

Protein-26g

Cholesterol-70mg

I'm not really sure which category to put this recipe in. I usually use them to put in sauce when I make spaghetti squash, but I recently added them to my tomato soup and they were amazing! So, I'll leave it up to you! This is one of those "be creative with these" recipes. This recipe is obviously high in protein and all the B vitamins.

Ingredients:
Olive oil spray
¾ lb ground turkey
¾ lb lean ground sirloin
2 egg whites
3 garlic cloves, minced
1 tsp dried oregano
1 tsp dried basil
2 tbs seasoned breadcrumbs
¼ c fresh parsley, chopped small
½ c minced onion
Lots of black pepper

Combine all ingredients in a large bowl. Shape the meat mixture into meatballs about 1 ½" in diameter. Place in a flat dish in one layer, as each is prepared. Spray a large, nonstick skillet with olive oil and place on medium-high heat. Add meatballs in batches, browning all over. Remove from pan and let cool.

Peach Salsa

Eggplant and Garlic Dip

Sauces, Dips and Salsas

"Statistics show that of those who contract the habit of eating, very few survive."
George Bernard Shaw, Irish playwright (1856-1950)

If I had a food nickname, it would be the "Condiment Kid." I admit it. I love sauces, salsas, anything you can come up with to put on meat, fish, chicken…or even veggies. I've heard that when you go into a high-end steak restaurant and order steak sauce, it's an insult to the chef. Ummm…I can only say, "I'M SORRY!" Evidently, I've managed to insult chefs in every major steak place in the United States…and a couple in Europe. So much for being politically correct. (Is this why the term "Ugly American" was invented?)

I would double the recipes here if I were you. You can freeze any extra, but it's doubtful you'll have any. I love mango, and the mango salsa recipe is one of my favorites. I use it on eggs, burgers, fish, or whatever I can think of. As for the dips, I am reminded of the story of when my sister-in-law went to a party and was asked if she brought the dip, to which she responded, "He's parking the car."

The eggplant and garlic dip goes great with cucumber slices or broiled chicken. You can even use it instead of ketchup. What a concept! There's more fiber, minerals and a LOT less sugar. It's really satisfying, too.

Roasted Red Pepper Tomato Sauce
Prep Time: 15 minutes
Cook Time: 1 hour
Serves 2

__Nutritional Facts:__

Calories-83

Total Fat-6g

Sat Fat-0g

Dietary Fiber-3g

Sugars-4g

Sodium- 16 mg

Total Carbohydrates-17g

Trans Fat-0g

Protein-3g

Cholesterol-0mg

Make a lot of this at one time and freeze it in small containers for future use. I do this with so many of the sauce recipes. Also, I don't really know how to cook for two. When I try, I end up with enough for about 17, so freezing is commonplace, but it makes it nice when you don't feel like cooking. This tomato sauce is a good source of fiber, vitamin D, thiamine, folate and potassium. The red pepper addition makes it very high in vitamin A, vitamin C, vitamin B6 and manganese.

Ingredients:

1 small head of garlic

½ lb roma tomatoes, halved lengthwise

1 large red bell pepper

Olive oil spray

1 ½ tsps fresh lemon juice

½ tsp balsamic vinegar

Pepper to taste

Preheat oven to 375 degrees. Cut off and discard top of garlic head and wrap remainder in foil. Arrange tomatoes, cut side up in an oil-sprayed, foil lined baking pan. Add whole bell pepper and garlic (in foil) to pan. Roast vegetables in middle of oven for 1 hour.

Transfer bell pepper to a bowl and cover bowl with plastic wrap. Let stand for about 20 minutes. When cool enough to touch, peel pepper, and discard stem and seeds and place in food processor along with the tomatoes. Unwrap garlic and squeeze into food processor. Add remaining ingredients, and puree until smooth.   Use as an accompaniment for turkey meatloaf or burgers.

Fun Food Tip: To easily remove burnt on food from your skillet, simply add a drop or two of dish soap and enough water to cover the bottom of the pan. Bring it to a boil on the stove. The skillet will be much easier to clean!

Fresh Mango Salsa
Prep Time: 15 minutes
Cook Time: Overnight
Serves 4

Nutritional Facts:

Calories: 36
Total Fat: 0g
Sat Fat: 1g
Dietary Fiber-1g
Sugars-5g

Sodium- 6mg
Total Carbohydrates-9g
Trans Fat-0g
Protein-1g
Cholesterol-0mg

Mango is my favorite fruit in the world. When I wanted to make a fruit salsa, it was an obvious choice. Make sure the mango is really ripe, as you'll need that sweetness to offset the onion. Have fun getting the last of the fruit off the seed with your teeth. (You're standing over the sink doing it, aren't you?) This salsa gives a ton of vitamin C and vitamin A. It also has vitamin K, vitamin B6, potassium, copper and manganese.

Ingredients:
2 cups roma tomatoes, seeded and diced
1 ½ cups diced, peeled mango
½ cup diced red onion
½ cup chopped fresh cilantro
2 Tbs lime juice
1 Tbs cider vinegar

Optional:
½ cup black beans, drained

Combine all ingredients in large bowl. Cover and let flavors blend overnight. Serve with fish or chicken.

Peach Salsa
Prep Time: 25 minutes
Cook Time: 5 minutes
Serves 4

Nutritional Facts:

Calories-26

Total Fat-0g

Sat Fat-0g

Dietary Fiber-1g

Sugars-5g

Sodium- 1 mg

Total Carbohydrates-6g

Trans Fat-0g

Protein-1g

Cholesterol-0mg

This version of fruit salsa is low in...well...everything! Isn't that great? I tried it with mango. Peach works better here. Again, the peaches MUST be ripe or the green and red pepper will overpower it. There's a lot of vitamin E, vitamin K, niacin, vitamin B6, potassium and manganese. It's also a very good source of vitamin A and vitamin C.

Ingredients:
3 ½ cups coarsely chopped peeled peaches
1 cup coarsely chopped red bell pepper
1 cup coarsely chopped green pepper
1/3 cup coarsely chopped red onion
1 jalapeno pepper, seeded and chopped
¼ cup fresh cilantro leaves
1 tbs limejuice.

Combine all ingredients in blender. Pulse until chopped small.

Basic Marinara Sauce
Prep Time: 10 minutes
Cook Time: 35 minutes
Serves 6

Nutritional Facts:

Calories-95
Total Fat-1g
Sat Fat-0g
Dietary Fiber-4g
Sugars-13g

Sodium- 336mg
Total Carbohydrates-22g
Trans Fat-0g
Protein-4g
Cholesterol-0mg

Every cookbook needs a basic marinara sauce. Feel free to add sautéed veggies, tofu, ground turkey, whatever you'd like to make it "yours." I often use this with spaghetti squash instead of pasta. It eats like pasta without all those nasty starchy carbs and calories! There's a lot of fiber, vitamin E, vitamin K, niacin, vitamin B6, magnesium and manganese. It's a very good source of vitamin A, vitamin C, iron, potassium and copper.

Ingredients:
Olive oil Spray
1/4 cup chopped onion
4 garlic cloves, thinly sliced
½ tsp dried basil
1/2 teaspoon black pepper
2 (14.5-ounce) cans diced tomatoes, undrained
1 (28-ounce) can crushed tomatoes, undrained
(for spicier sauce, add ½ tsp red pepper flakes)

Spray and heat oil in a saucepan over medium-high heat. Add onion and garlic. Cook 3 minutes or until tender; stir constantly. Stir in remaining ingredients; bring to a boil. Reduce heat; simmer 30 minutes. Serve.

Fun Food Tip: Spray your plastic storage containers with cooking spray before pouring in tomato sauces. They won't stain.

Black Bean Confetti Relish

Prep Time: 10 minutes
Cook Time: 3 minutes
Serves 4

Nutritional Facts:

Calories-142

Total Fat-3g

Sat Fat-0g

Dietary Fiber-6g

Sugars-4g

Sodium- 8 mg

Total Carbohydrates-24g

Trans Fat-0g

Protein-6g

Cholesterol-0mg

Know what my secret is with this? I use it in my Mexican-style turkey meatloaf! I add about ½-3/4 cup of this to my meat, depending on how many pounds I'm making, along with a little tomato sauce and spices and WHAM! Instant hit. It's also good with chips. It has lots of fiber, folate and manganese and a very good source of vitamin C. (nutritional facts are for ½ the recipe)

Ingredients:

2/3 cup canned black beans, rinsed and drained
2 tablespoons frozen whole-kernel corn
2 tablespoons diced yellow bell pepper
2 tablespoons diced plum tomato
1 tablespoon diced red bell pepper
1 tablespoon minced shallots
1 tablespoon lemon juice
1 teaspoon olive oil
1/4 teaspoon ground cumin
1/4 teaspoon coarsely ground black pepper

Combine all the ingredients in a bowl. Serve relish chilled or at room temperature.

Caramelized-Onion Sauce
Prep Time: 10 minutes
Cook Time: 30 minutes
Serves 4

Nutritional Facts:

Calories-115

Total Fat-1g

Sat Fat-0g

Dietary Fiber-2g

Sugars-4g

Sodium- 60 mg

Total Carbohydrates-12g

Trans Fat-0g

Protein-5g

Cholesterol-0mg

This sauce makes for a nice side dish with pasta when you're making fish or chicken. You can even use it as a steak sauce! I like a lot of pepper. It's very low in cholesterol and sodium.

Ingredients:

Butter flavored oil spray

3 cups thinly sliced onion

1 cup dry red wine

3 cups fat-free, less-sodium chicken broth

1/8 teaspoon black pepper

Spray oil in a large skillet over medium-high heat. Add onion; cook 5 minutes, stirring frequently. Continue cooking 15 minutes or until deep golden brown, stirring constantly. Add wine; cook 5 minutes or until liquid almost evaporates. Remove onion from pan; finely chop them and return to pan. Stir in broth and pepper. Bring to a boil. Cook until reduced to 2 cups (about 10 minutes).

Eggplant and Garlic Dip
Prep Time: 10 minutes
Cook Time: about 1 ½ hours
Serves 4

Nutritional Facts:

Calories-22

Total Fat-0g

Sat Fat-0g

Dietary Fiber-2g

Sugars-2g

Sodium- 5 mg

Total Carbohydrates-5g

Trans Fat-0g

Protein-1g

Cholesterol-0mg

This version of babaganoush is very low fat. It takes a little bit of time, but whenever I've served this to guests, they love it. You can use either pita bread cut in triangles or crudités. I love it with red pepper slices. Yum! It's a good source of vitamin K, folate, magnesium, phosphorus and copper. Lots of fiber, vitamin C, vitamin B6, potassium and manganese, too.

Ingredients:

1 eggplant, about 1 1/2 pounds

1 head garlic

2 tbs balsamic vinegar

1/4 cup chopped basil or parsley

2-3 tbs nonfat yogurt

Pepper to taste

2 tsp lemon juice

Preheat oven to 350 degrees. Cut slits in eggplant(s). Place in a shallow roasting pan or on a cookie sheet. You can put your garlic on the same pan after cutting the tops off and wrapping it in tin foil. Bake garlic and eggplant until eggplant wrinkles and starts to collapse; about 1 to 1.25 hours. Remove from oven. Allow to cool enough to be able to touch. Slice open eggplant and scrape pulp into bowl of food processor. Squeeze garlic pulp into processor bowl too. Add the vinegar, lemon juice, basil or parsley, yogurt and pepper. Process until mix is fairly smooth but still a little chunky. Alternatively, chop eggplant pulp with a knife and mix with other ingredients.

Makes about 2 cups.

Mutabbel
Eggplant Dip with Tahini – crushed Sesame Seeds
Prep Time: 30 minutes
Cook Time: 10 minutes
Serves 8

Nutritional Facts:

Calories: 76

Total Fat: 3g

Sat Fat: 0g

Dietary Fiber-6g

Sugars-4g

Sodium- 8 mg

Total Carbohydrates-12g

Trans Fat-0g

Protein-2g

Cholesterol-0mg

I got this recipe from my friend, Chef Michael Bowen, who specializes in fast and healthy food. He had to *physically* hold me back from this dish, as I'm a big fan of eggplant…and there were other people at the party.   This food is very low in cholesterol and sodium. It is also a good source of vitamin K, vitamin B6, folate, potassium and copper, and a very good source of dietary fiber, vitamin C and manganese.

Ingredients:

3 large eggplants – split in ½ and lightly brushed with olive oil

6 large garlic cloves – roasted for about ½ hour to a light brown in a 350 degree oven.

1 tablespoon tahini

2 lemons zested, then juiced – strain seeds and pulp

1 jalapeño pepper – ribs and seeds cleaned out and finely diced

½ tsp chili powder

½ tsp ground cumin

2 tbs good olive oil

Split the eggplants in half and brush the flesh very lightly (not skin) with olive oil. Roast flat side down on a medium hot wood fire (Always preferred over gas, but who can argue with the ease?) until slightly charred. You can roast them in the oven, too, at about 400-425 degrees. Finish roasting on the BBQ when the fire dies down with cover on or just in your 350-degree oven. The flesh should be very soft and almost falling off the skin when done.   Scoop flesh out of skin and discard the skin.

Place all ingredients into a food processor or electric blender and blend to a smooth consistency.   Pour onto a serving dish and serve with accoutrements: Garnish with a sprinkle of smoked paprika, chopped fresh parsley and kalamata olives

Serve with warm flat or toasted whole wheat Pita Breads or Crudité.

Compuesta Dip
Prep Time: ½ hour
Serves 10-ish

Nutritional Facts:

Calories: 134

Total Fat: 3g

Sat Fat: 1g

Dietary Fiber-6g

Sugars-6g

Sodium- 157 mg

Total Carbohydrates-20g

Trans Fat-0g

Protein-8g

Cholesterol-2mg

Notice I have no cook time here. Since all you have to do is chop, sprinkle and mix, there's really no "cooking." It was hard to figure out the serving size, as I could eat the entire thing myself. But, as it's a party dip, to be served with fresh crudités or baked chips, I've divided it into *human* portions. The avocado is the only thing that has any fat, but it's very healthy, important fat. This is high in fiber and omega-6 fatty acids. I never have any leftover with this. You can also cheat a little with this recipe and use one package of taco seasoning instead of the separate spices. I'm wary of these, though, as they're often really high in sodium and chemicals I can't pronounce.

Ingredients:

2 cans of low salt, fat free re-fried beans or black beans

1 medium onion, chopped

1 medium avocado, mashed

½ cup corn

12 oz low salt salsa

1 c organic non-fat yogurt

1 tbs chili powder

1 1/2 tsp cumin

1 tsp each: dried cilantro, onion, garlic and oregano

1/2-cup low fat Monterrey jack or sharp cheddar cheese

3 medium tomatoes, chopped

Mix the two cans of beans with the chopped onion. Spread in a 2 quart pyrex dish. Then, take the avocado, corn and salsa and place all in a bowl. Mix well and spread over the beans and onion. In another bowl, mix the yogurt and spices together and spread over the avocado/salsa mixture. Lastly, sprinkle the top with the cheese and tomatoes.

Serve with slices of red and green pepper and cucumbers or baked corn chips (if you MUST!).

Apple Brown Betty

Creamy Ice
Banana

Desserts

"Seize the moment. Remember all those women on the Titanic who waved off the dessert cart."
Erma Bombeck

Really!? Do I have to write an introduction? It's **DESSERT** for goodness sake! I bet you thought that because this is a healthy cookbook, it wouldn't have any, didn't you? Now, realize these recipes are a better choice than regular desserts, but they still should be eaten as a treat only once in a while. Too much of anything isn't good for you.

Except shoes. One can NEVER have enough shoes!! (And shoes are fewer calories. You don't eat them.)

The Apple Brown Betty is a great re-engineered recipe from a classic dessert. It's one of my favorites. The crunch and the sweetness are really satisfying. I actually like it as a topping for low-fat coffee flavored frozen yogurt or no-sugar ice cream. Or, to be really decadent, heat it up and put the frozen yogurt on top of it!

There! Don't you feel better? Your favorite part of the meal can still be included in a healthful diet! My work here is finished. Whew! After all this writing about food, I'm getting hungry. I'll be in the kitchen, working on recipes for my next cookbook...and sampling everything, of course!

Apple Brown Betty

Prep Time: 15 minutes
Cook Time: 1 hour
Serves 6

Nutritional Facts:

Calories-379

Total Fat-6g

Sat Fat-2g

Dietary Fiber-7g

Sugars-48g

Sodium- 141 mg

Total Carbohydrates-81g

Trans Fat-0g

Protein-6g

Cholesterol-0mg

The sugars here are all from the fruits and juices used. No refined sugar here! As desserts go, anything apple is always popular. This just makes it a little healthier, too! It's a good source of vitamin C, iron and manganese.

Ingredients:

6 Golden Delicious apples, sliced to about ½"

3/4 cup frozen apple juice concentrate,

1/2 cup golden raisins

1 teaspoon ground cinnamon

3 tablespoon plus 1/3 cup whole-wheat flour

1/3 cup quick oats

2 packets of stevia

3 tablespoon Smart Balance butter substitute, melted

Preheat oven to 375°F. Coat and 11-inch by 7-inch baking dish with nonstick spray. Set aside. In a large bowl, combine the apples, apple juice concentrate, raisins, cinnamon, and 3 tablespoons of the flour. Spoon into the prepared dish.

In a medium bowl, combine the oats, stevia, Smart Balance, and the remaining 1/3 cup of flour. Stir to mix until crumbly. Sprinkle over the apple mixture. Bake for 1 hour, or until bubbly and golden brown. Serve warm.

Broiled Peaches and Strawberries
Prep Time: 10 minutes
Cook Time: 5 minutes
Serves 6

Nutritional Facts:

Calories-80

Total Fat-1g

Sat Fat-0g

Dietary Fiber-4g

Sugars-15g

Sodium- 1 mg

Total Carbohydrates-19g

Trans Fat-0g

Protein-1g

Cholesterol-0mg

A simple, yet flavorful dessert, this will satisfy those with a sweet tooth very well. It's low in calories, a good source of fiber, vitamin A, potassium, vitamin C and manganese.

Ingredients:

5 medium peaches, sliced

1 1/2 pint strawberries, halved

1 packet stevia

1/2 teaspoon ground cinnamon

1/2 teaspoon ground allspice or cloves

Butter flavored cooking spray

3 tablespoon slivered fresh mint

Preheat the broiler. Coat a large baking sheet with sides with cooking spray.
In a large bowl, combine the peaches, strawberries, stevia, cinnamon, and allspice or cloves and toss to coat well. Place the fruit on the prepared baking sheet. Spray with butter spray.

Broil, turning the pan 2 or 3 times (no need to turn the fruit), for 4 minutes, or until the fruit is glazed, bubbly, and golden brown in spots. Remove from the oven and let cool slightly.

Sprinkle with the mint. Serve warm or at room temperature.

Chocolate Cheesecake
Prep Time: 25 minutes
Cook Time: About 2 hours
Serves 10

Nutritional Facts:

Calories: 239

Total Fat: 13g

Sat Fat: 5g

Dietary Fiber-1g

Sugars-6g

Sodium- 253 mg

Total Carbohydrates-21g

Trans Fat-0g

Protein-9g

Cholesterol-95mg

You looked at this recipe hoping it would be ridiculously low in calories, didn't you? Trust me. Any cheesecake worth eating has calories. I just re-worked this one so one slice didn't equal a full day's worth.

Ingredients:
1 lb (2 - 8 oz. packages) low fat cream cheese
4 oz. dark chocolate, finely chopped
1 ts. cocoa
5 packets Stevia
3 tsp vanilla extract
3 eggs
3 C fat free sour cream

Preheat oven to 375° F. Finely chop chocolate in a food processor or use a knife. Set aside. In a large bowl, beat cream cheese and sweeteners until smooth, add eggs one at a time, beating after each addition. Add vanilla and finely chopped chocolate, and then beat in the sour cream just until blended. Put in a pre-formed pan. Bake for 50-60 minutes, depending on your oven and how brown the top gets. Then turn off oven and don't open the door for another hour. Remove from oven, cool and then chill completely before serving.

Chocolate-Glazed Pears

Preparation Time: 30 mins
Cooking Time: 10 mins
Serves 6
Extra Time: 20 mins (for cooling and setting)

Nutritional Facts:

Calories-264
Total Fat-9g
Sat Fat-5g
Dietary Fiber-7g
Sugars-32g

Sodium- 32 mg
Total Carbohydrates-46g
Trans Fat-0g
Protein-2g
Cholesterol-1mg

The best for this recipe are the comice pears. They're juicy and flavorful and work very well with the chocolate. (Let's face it...there's CHOCOLATE here...if you ask me, it works with anything...I'd eat it with cauliflower if needed!) It also has good fiber. Hey, I had to add *something* here....

Ingredients:

3 cups water
4 packets of stevia
1 lemon peel twist (2-inch)
6 USA Bosc pears
6 oz semi-sweet baking chocolate
2 Tbsp Smart Balance butter spread

Combine water, stevia and lemon twist in a saucepan; bring to a boil. Pare pears and trim slightly to level bottom; core pears, leaving stem intact. Add pears to poaching liquid; reduce heat. Cover and simmer gently about 8 to 10 minutes or until tender when pierced with tip of sharp knife; turn and baste occasionally.
Remove pears from liquid; stand them on flat dish to cool. Melt chocolate and Smart Balance over very low heat. Dry pears completely with paper towels. Holding each pear carefully by the stem, spoon or drip chocolate mixture over pear to coat. Let stand in cool place to set chocolate. Arrange pears on serving dish.

Summer Fruit Salad
Prep Time: 15 minutes
Cook Time: 5 minutes
Serves 4

<u>*Nutritional Facts:*</u>

Calories: 100

Total Fat: 3g

Sat Fat: 3g

Dietary Fiber-3g

Sugars-14g

Sodium- 1 mg

Total Carbohydrates-18g

Trans Fat-0g

Protein-2g

Cholesterol-0mg

Easy and pretty, it takes no time and is a light, refreshing end to any summer barbeque. It's a good source of fiber, vitamin E, vitamin K and manganese, as well as vitamin C.

Ingredients:
1 cup mixed berries
1 mango peeled, pitted and cubed
1 nectarine pitted and sliced
2 tbs orange juice

Optional:
Add ¼ cup sliced almonds

Mix the fruit in a bowl. Sprinkle with the orange juice. Serve for breakfast over yogurt, as a side dish with lunch or dinner, or for dessert over sorbet.

Apple Pie à la Mode Parfaits
Prep Time: 25 minutes
Cook Time: 1 hour, 15 minutes
Serves 8

Nutritional Facts:

Calories-173

Total Fat-7g

Sat Fat: 3g

Dietary Fiber-2g

Sugars-10g

Sodium- 92 mg

Total Carbohydrates-29g

Trans Fat-0g

Protein-3g

Cholesterol-14mg

This is your official "cheat" dessert. It has cookies and ice cream in it. So, it's not perfect. Just enjoy it…but only every so often, please! Try it at a family dinner. The fat grams aren't out of sight and your kids will never know!

Ingredients:

4 1/2 cups chopped peeled cooking apple (such as Cortlands)

1/2 cup Splenda

1 tablespoon fresh lemon juice

1 teaspoon apple-pie spice

½ teaspoon cinnamon

3 cups no sugar, low fat oatmeal cookie crumbs, (about 4 ounces, crushed)

3 cups vanilla low-fat, no sugar ice cream, softened

Combine the first 5 ingredients in a medium saucepan, and bring to a boil. Cover, reduce heat, and simmer 5 minutes. Uncover; simmer 5 minutes or until tender, stirring occasionally. Spoon into a bowl; cover and chill for one hour. Spoon 1-tablespoon cookie crumbs into each of 8 (8-ounce) glasses; top each with 1/4 cup apple mixture and 3 tablespoons ice cream. Repeat the layers once, ending with ice cream. Serve immediately.

Creamy Ice Banana
Prep Time: 8 minutes
Freezer Time: 2 Hours
Cook Time: 2 minutes
Serves 4

Nutritional Facts:

Calories: 169
Total Fat: 3g
Sat Fat: 0g
Dietary Fiber-5g
Sugars-19g

Sodium- 2 mg
Total Carbohydrates-36g
Trans Fat-0g
Protein-3g
Cholesterol-0mg

My Mom used to make a version of this, except they were logs. For those, cut a ripe banana into 1 ½" slices, dip in orange juice, then roll into crushed walnuts or almonds. Place on a baking sheet and freeze for 2 hours. Easy to eat with a fork or toothpicks! This is a good source of fiber, vitamin C, vitamin B6 and manganese.

Ingredients:
4 very ripe large bananas. (With brown speckles. Any more, banana becomes too ripe)

Peel the bananas and slice them into ½ inch thick rounds. Place the slices on a baking sheet. Freeze bananas for 2 hours. In a food processor or blender, puree frozen banana slices until creamy. Stop occasionally to scrape side of machine. Serve immediately.

Optional: Sprinkle with sliced almonds and cinnamon. (And if you want to splurge…chocolate sprinkles!)

"Never eat more than you can lift."
Miss Piggy

Fun and Easy Home Remedy Tips
I'm no Heloise, but I thought these would be helpful!

1. To get rid of the itch from a mosquito bite, apply soap on it. Instant relief!

2. Try using air freshener to clean your mirrors, it does a good job and better still, leaves a nice smell.

3. When you get a splinter, try scotch tape before resorting to tweezers or a needle. Simple put the tape over the splinter and pull it off.

4. If the scotch tape doesn't work, try Elmer's Glue! Pour it over the splinter, let it dry and peel the dried glue off the skin. The splinter sticks to the dried glue.

5. A new use for alka-seltzer—cleaner! Drop two tablets into your toilet. Wait 20 minutes, brush and flush. The citric acid and effervescent action clean vitreous china.

 Do the same with a vase or cruet.... fill with water; use two tablets, brush and rinse.

Want to polish your jewelry? Alka-seltzer again! Put two tablets in a large glass of water. Immerse your jewelry for about 2 minutes. Sparkling!

How about a thermos? Fill the bottle with water, drop in 4 tablets and let it soak for about an hour. Brush and rinse.

You can even unclog your drain. Drop 3 A-S tablets down the drain followed by a cup of white vinegar. Wait a few minutes, and then run your hot water.

Cure urinary tract infections with Alka Seltzer.   Just dissolve two tablets in a glass of water and drink it at the onset of the symptoms. It begins to eliminate the infection almost immediately, although the product was never advertised for this use.

6. Colgate toothpaste makes an excellent salve for burns.

7. Stuffed nose? Try sucking on an Altoids peppermint. That'll clear it!

8. The flu can cause achy muscles. Mix one tablespoon of white horseradish with ½ cup of olive oil. Let it sit for about ½ hour and apply it as massage oil for relief.

9. An old model's trick for eliminating under eye puffiness; Preparation H. Carefully rub it into the skin under your eyes. It acts as a vasoconstrictor, relieving the swelling instantly.

10. Get rid of toenail fungus by soaking your toes in Listerine mouthwash. The antiseptic leaves your toenails looking healthy again.

Quotes and Quips from my (so-called) Friends!

"I don't usually eat anything that's good for me but I would eat everything in this book!"
Bobby Caravella...Restaurateur, Raconteur

"Don't worry Rona! We've all had worse things in our mouths before!"
Jim Michaels, Co-Executive Producer, "Everybody Hates Chris"

I love Rona, her training AND her food. Finally, I can get what I need from her book and shut her up whenever I want by closing the cover. Thing is, you won't want to. Besides her yummy and EASY recipes, her stories are hilarious and you'll wanna read 'em when marinating your chicken, waiting for the soup to boil OR if you are having a bad day and just need a lift. The book is more than recipes. It's like having your favorite gal pal (or trainer/chef) whenever you need her.
Laurie Searle, Owner   www.YogaAndFitnessToGo.com

If you aren't lucky enough to have Rona cook for you, this is the second best option. Rona's food goes from yummy to yummier!
Donna N., New York City, long time (but not old) friend of Rona

"A wise saying is, 'if you want to be rich – do what the rich people do!' No less wise is the suggestion that to look and act terrific, you have to do what the terrific do! Except for bicycle shorts.... wait before you wear the bicycle shorts.
Ed Stanley, Georgia Jet, Inc.

"When Rona's cooking, it's not only the kitchen that's hot!"
Brian Reeves, friend and fellow actor

"I read this book and laughed so hard the neighbors had to call the police!"
James @ January Project

I've seen you eat and I've seen how thin and fit you are...it is about time you put your 'secret' recipes into a cookbook so the rest of us can look that good!
Joan Forder, Ph. D.   www.joanforder.ca

INDEX

A

Al dente, 4
Allergies, 11, 14
Allspice
    Beef with Lebanese Spices, Ground, 116
    Peaches and Strawberries, Broiled, 141
Almonds, 9, 15
    Creamy Ice Banana, 146
    Fruit Salad, Summer, 144
    Outrageous Oatmeal, 24, 34
    Power Muffins, 33
Alpha-linoleic acid (ALA), 12, 16
Anemia, 11
Anise, 11
Anti-cancer, 11–14, 16
Anti-coagulant, 12
Anti-inflammatory, 11–12, 17
Anti-microbial agent, 12
Anti-oxidant, 12, 16, 22
Antibacterial, 11–12, 14
Antifungal, 11, 14
Antihistamine, 11
Antioxidants, 12, 14–16, 22
Antispasmodic, 13
Anxiety, 13, 18
Apples, 20
    Apple Brown Betty, 137, 139–40
    Apple Pie à la Mode Parfaits, 145
Applesauce
    Power Muffins, 33
Arthritis, 11–12
Asparagus, 20
    Frittata, Asparagus and Leek, 29
    Omelet, Herbed Asparagus, 30
    Quiche, Vegetable Breakfast, 31–32
Asthma, 11–12, 14
Avocado, 15, 20
    Compuesta Dip, 136

B

Bad breath, 11–12
Baking, 4
Balsamic vinegar
    Chicken with Peppers, 114
    Dip, Eggplant and Garlic, 126, 134
    Marinated Zucchini, 77
    Pepper Sauté, Italian, 78
    Red Peppers, Roasted, 73
    Sauce, Roasted Red Pepper Tomato, 128
    Skirt Steak, Marinated, 119
    Soup, Lentil Spinach, 58
    Veal Stew with Tomatoes and Balsamic Vinegar, 88
    Yellow Tomatoes in Balsamic Vinaigrette, 72
Bananas, 18
    Creamy Ice Banana, 138, 146
    Outrageous Oatmeal, 24, 34
    Power Muffins, 33
Basil, 9, 11
    Beef Burgers, Italian-Style, 120
    Chicken Florentine Soup, 64
    Chicken Pesto, 113
    Chili-1 skillet meal, Quick Italian, 105
    Eggplant and Garlic Dip, 126, 134
    Gazpacho, 60
    Meatballs, Lean, 124
    Minestrone, 57
    Mushrooms in Lemon Marinade, 68, 76
    Sauce, Basic Marinara, 131
    Tofu Salad, 46
    Tomato and Zucchini Salad, 39
    Tomato Soup with Roasted Peppers, 51
    Trout, Poached, 100
    Vegetable Breakfast Quiche, 31–32
    Vegetables with Italian-Style Turkey Sausage, Oven Roasted, 104
    Zucchini, Marinated, 77
Beans, 9
    Beans with Kale, Stewed, 70
    Black Bean Confetti Relish, 132
    Compuesta Dip, 136
    Haricots Verts with Garlic, 79
    Oven Roasted Vegetables with Italian-Style Turkey Sausage, 104
    Soup, Southwest Shrimp, 55
    Turkey Chili, 106
    Vegetarian Chili, 123
Beef
    Beef Burgers, Italian-Style, 120
    Ground Beef with Lebanese Spices, 116
    Marinated Beef for Fajitas, Tequila, 115
    Marinated Skirt Steak, 119
    Meatballs, Lean, 124
    Soup, Mom's Garbage, 49, 65–66
Beef broth
    Soup, Mom's Garbage, 49, 65–66
    Veal Stew with Tomatoes and Balsamic Vinegar, 88
Bell peppers, 20
Beta-carotene, 16

Black beans, 15
    Black Bean Confetti Relish, 132
    Compuesta Dip, 136
    Fresh Mango Salsa, 129
    Vegetarian Chili, 123
Black olives
    Green Beans Provençal, 80
Blanching, 4
Blood
    clotting, 12, 22
    pressure, 12–13, 16, 21
    purifier, 16
    sugar regulation, 11
Blueberries, 15, 20
    Outrageous Oatmeal, 24, 34
    Power Muffins, 33
Bluefish, 20
Boiling, 4
Bok choy
    Asian Style Foil Fish, 94
Bones, 16, 21
Braising, 4
Breakfast
    Burritos, Egg, Mushroom & Roasted Red
        Pepper, 23, 27
    Frittata, Asparagus and Leek, 29
    Omelet, Deviled Crab Egg White, 26
    Omelet, Herbed Asparagus, 30
    Omelet with Summer Vegetables, 28
    Outrageous Oatmeal, 24, 34
    Power Muffins, 33
    Quiche, Vegetable Breakfast, 31–32
Breast cancer, 16
Broccoli, 15
    Broccoli Soup, 63
    Minestrone, 57
    Vegetable Breakfast Quiche, 31–32
Broiling, 4
Bronchitis, 12, 14
Brown rice, 69
    Baked Chicken with Wild Rice, 109
    Garbanzos with Spinach, 84
    Oven Roasted Vegetables with Italian-Style
        Turkey Sausage, 104
Brussels Sprouts, 15
Bunch, 8

C
Cabbage
    Asian Slaw, 44
    Soup, Mom's Garbage, 49, 65–66

    Soup, Spicy Red Pepper, 47, 53
Caffeinated beverages, 19
Calcium, 15, 17, 21
Capsaicin, 18
Caraway, 11
Cardamom, 11
Carrots
    Asian Slaw, 44
    Minestrone, 57
    Quiche, Vegetable Breakfast, 31–32
    Salad, Moroccan Carrot, 41
    Salad, Tofu, 46
    Soup, Mom's Garbage, 49, 65–66
    Stock, Wild Mushroom, 50
    Zucchini and Carrots with Fresh Mint or
        Parsley, 67, 71
Cayenne pepper, 9, 11
    Gazpacho, 60
    Pork Fajitas with Pan Roasted Peppers, 121
    Salad, Moroccan Carrot, 41
Celery
    Lentil Spinach Soup, 58
    Minestrone, 57
    Shrimp in New Orleans Sauce, 101
Chamomile, 11
Cheese. *See also* cream cheese; feta cheese; goat
    cheese; Parmesan cheese
    Burritos, Egg, Mushroom & Roasted Red
        Pepper, 23, 27
    Compuesta Dip, 136
    Frittata, Asparagus and Leek, 29
    Omelet, Herbed Asparagus, 30
    Omelet with Summer Vegetables, 28
    Quiche, Vegetable Breakfast, 31–32
    Tomato Soup with Roasted Peppers, 51
Cherries, 20
Chick peas
    Minestrone, 57
Chicken, 18
    Baked Chicken with Wild Rice, 109
    Basic Sauté of Chicken and Herbs, 107
    Chicken, Oriental Grilled, 111
    Chicken Breasts with Peppers, 108
    Chicken Florentine Soup, 64
    Chicken in Red Wine Sauce, 112
    Chicken Pesto, 113
    Chicken Sausage, Ratatouille with, 110
    Chicken Sausage, Spicy Kale Chowder with,
        54
    Chicken with Peppers, 114

Italian-Style Turkey Sausage, Oven Roasted
  Vegetables with, 104
Tequila Marinated Beef for Fajitas, 115
Chicken stock
  Baked Chicken with Wild Rice, 109
  Basic Sauté of Chicken and Herbs, 107
  Braised Mixed Bell Peppers, 83
  Chicken in Red Wine Sauce, 112
  Chicken with Peppers, 114
  Chowder with Chicken Sausage, Spicy Kale,
    54
  Frittata, Asparagus and Leek, 29
  Lamb with Tarragon, Boneless Loin of, 90
  Mushrooms in Lemon Marinade, 68, 76
  Sauce, Caramelized-Onion, 133
  Soup, Broccoli, 63
  Soup, Chicken Florentine, 64
  Soup, Cold Cream of Cucumber, 48, 62
  Soup, Cucumber Mint, 61
  Soup with Roasted Peppers, Tomato, 51
  Stir-Fried Pea Shoots and Shiitakes with
    Shrimp, 93
Chili flakes
  Asian Style Foil Fish, 94
  Vegetable Breakfast Quiche, 31–32
Chili oil, 10
Chili pepper
  Salad, Tomato and Sweet Pepper, 40
  Soup, Spicy Red Pepper, 47, 53
Chili powder
  Baked Chicken with Wild Rice, 109
  Chili, Turkey, 106
  Chili, Vegetarian, 123
  Compuesta Dip, 136
  Mutabbel (eggplant), 135
  Omelet with Summer Vegetables, 28
  Shrimp, South of the Border, 102
  Shrimp Soup, Southwest, 55
Chili sauce
  Turkey Chili, 106
Chives, 11
  Frittata, Asparagus and Leek, 29
  Poached Trout, 100
  Soup, Cold Cream of Cucumber, 48, 62
Chocolate, 15
  Chocolate Cheesecake, 142
  Chocolate Glazed Pears, 143
Cholesterol, 13
Cholesterol reduction, 12–13, 15–16
Cider vinegar
  Salsa, Fresh Mango, 129

Soup, Hot and Sour, 59
Cilantro, 9
  Baked Chicken with Wild Rice, 109
  Chili, Turkey, 106
  Chili, Vegetarian, 123
  Compuesta Dip, 136
  Grilled Shrimp with Thai Lemongrass
    Marinade, 97
  Marinated Skirt Steak, 119
  Omelet, Deviled Crab Egg White, 26
  Pork Fajitas with Pan Roasted Peppers, 121
  Salad, Heirloom Tomato, Lime and Onion, 42
  Salad, Tofu, 46
  Salsa, Fresh Mango, 129
  Salsa, Peach, 125, 130
  Soup, Southwest Shrimp, 55
Cinnamon, 9, 11–12
  Apple Brown Betty, 137, 139–40
  Apple Pie à la Mode Parfaits, 145
  Ground Beef with Lebanese Spices, 116
  Ice Banana, Creamy, 138, 146
  Lamb and Eggplant, Casserole of, 89
  Outrageous Oatmeal, 24, 34
  Peaches and Strawberries, Broiled, 141
  Power Muffins, 33
Cleanup tools, 7
Cloves, 12
  Peaches and Strawberries, Broiled, 141
  Spicy Kale Chowder with Chicken Sausage,
    54
  Spicy Red Pepper Soup, 47, 53
Cocoa
  Chocolate Cheesecake, 142
Cod, 20
Coffee, 19
Coho Salmon, 20
Colds, 11
Colon cancer, 14
Concentration, 13
Congestion, 11
Cooking equipment, 6
Cooking techniques, 4–5
Copper, 21
Coriander, 9
  Cherry Tomatoes with Watermelon, 35, 45
  Grilled Shrimp with Thai Lemongrass
    Marinade, 97
Corn
  Black Bean Confetti Relish, 132
  Compuesta Dip, 136
  Omelet with Summer Vegetables, 28

Tofu Salad, 46
Coronary-artery disease, 16
Coughs, 11–12
Crabmeat
    Deviled Crab Egg White Omelet, 26
Cramps, 11
Crankiness, 18
Cream cheese. *See also* cheese
    Chocolate Cheesecake, 142
Cucumber, 20
    Gazpacho, 60
    Salmon with Cucumber Sauce, Poached, 99
    Soup, Cold Cream of Cucumber, 48, 62
    Soup, Cucumber Mint, 61
Cumin, 9
    Beef with Lebanese Spices, Ground, 116
    Black Bean Confetti Relish, 132
    Chicken with Wild Rice, Baked, 109
    Compuesta Dip, 136
    Garbanzos with Spinach, 84
    Gazpacho, 60
    Moroccan Carrot Salad, 41
    Mutabbel (eggplant), 135
    Pork Medallions with Herb Marinade, Grilled, 92
    Salad, Tomato and Sweet Pepper, 40
    Salad, Watercress and Orange, 36, 38
    Shrimp, South of the Border, 102
    Shrimp Soup, Southwest, 55
    Tequila Marinated Beef for Fajitas, 115
    Turkey Chili, 106
    Yellow Tomatoes in Balsamic Vinaigrette, 72
Curry, 9, 12

D
Dash, 8
Dehydration, 19
Depression, 18
Desserts
    Apple Brown Betty, 137, 139–40
    Apple Pie à la Mode Parfaits, 145
    Chocolate Cheesecake, 142
    Chocolate Glazed Pears, 143
    Creamy Ice Banana, 138, 146
    Fruit Salad, Summer, 144
    Peaches and Strawberries, Broiled, 141
Diabetes, 11–13, 21
Diarrhea, 13
Dice, 4
Digestive aid, 11–12
Digestive disorders, 11

Dijon mustard
    Marinated Skirt Steak, 119
    Watercress and Orange Salad, 36, 38
Dill, 9, 12
    Omelet, Deviled Crab Egg White, 26
    Poached Salmon with Cucumber Sauce, 99
    Poached Trout, 100
    Ratatouille, 74
    Soup, Cold Cream of Cucumber, 48, 62
    Soup, Mom's Garbage, 49, 65–66
    Soup, Sweet Pepper, 52
Dilute, 4
Dips. *See* sauces, dips and salsas
Diuretic, 13
Dizziness, 12
Drain, 4
Dry measurements, 8

E
Egg
    Chocolate Cheesecake, 142
    Egg, Mushroom & Roasted Red Pepper Burritos, 23, 27
    Omelet, Herbed Asparagus, 30
    Omelet with Summer Vegetables, 28
    Quiche, Vegetable Breakfast, 31–32
Egg whites
    Burritos, Egg, Mushroom & Roasted Red Pepper, 23, 27
    Chicken Pesto, 113
    Frittata, Asparagus and Leek, 29
    Meatballs, Lean, 124
    Omelet, Deviled Crab Egg White, 26
    Omelet, Herbed Asparagus, 30
    Omelet with Summer Vegetables, 28
    Quiche, Vegetable Breakfast, 31–32
    Soup, Hot and Sour, 59
    Stir-Fried Pea Shoots and Shiitakes with Shrimp, 93
Egg yolks
    Frittata, Asparagus and Leek, 29
Eggplant
    Eggplant and Garlic Dip, 126, 134
    Eggplant Salad, Grilled, 43
    Lamb and Eggplant, Casserole of, 89
    Mutabbel, 135
    Oven-Baked Mixed Vegetables, 75
    Oven Roasted Vegetables with Italian-Style Turkey Sausage, 104
    Ratatouille, 74
    Ratatouille with Chicken Sausage, 110

Endive
    Watercress and Orange Salad, 36, 38
Endorphins, 18
Essential fats, 16
Estrogen metabolism, 16
Expectorant, 13
Eyesight, 16

F
Fat-burning, 11, 21
Fennel, 12
Fennel seeds
    Quick Italian Chili-1 skillet meal, 105
Feta cheese. *See also* cheese
    Asparagus and Leek Frittata, 29
Fiber, 15–16, 21
Figs, 15
Fish, 20
    Asian Style Foil Fish, 94
    Fish Fillets in Foil, 85, 96
    Salmon and White Bean Salad, Grilled, 117
    Salmon with Cucumber Sauce, Poached, 99
    Trout, Poached, 100
Fish oil, 16
Fish stock
    Salmon with Cucumber Sauce, Poached, 99
Flavonoids, 15
Flax seed
    Power Muffins, 33
Flaxseed, 12, 16
Folate, 15, 21
Free-radicals, 22
Fruit, 20
Fun food tip
    arthritis pain and oatmeal, 34
    burnt skillet cleaning, 128
    celery in refrigerator, 45
    eggshell, preventing cracked, 32
    fresh eggs, 26
    headache and lime cure, 42
    honey and skin blemishes, 115
    jar opening, 81
    lemon juice, 76
    potato budding, 88
    potatoes and stains, 94
    tomato sauce stains, 131
    white vinegar and bruises, 77
    wine, freezing leftover, 70

G
Garam Masala, 9

Garbanzo beans
    Garbanzos with Spinach, 84
Garlic, 10, 12
    Braised Mixed Bell Peppers, 83
    Broiled Tomatoes, 82
    Cherry Tomatoes with Garlic and Parsley, 81
    Chicken Pesto, 113
    Chili-1 skillet meal, Quick Italian, 105
    Dip, Eggplant and Garlic, 126, 134
    Fish, Asian Style Foil, 94
    Garbanzos with Spinach, 84
    Gazpacho, 60
    Green Beans Provençal, 80
    Haricots Verts with Garlic, 79
    Lamb and Eggplant, Casserole of, 89
    Lamb Chops, Herb-Marinated, 118
    Marinade, Grilled Shrimp with Thai
        Lemongrass, 97
    Marinated Beef for Fajitas, Tequila, 115
    Marinated Skirt Steak, 119
    Marinated Zucchini, 77
    Meatballs, Lean, 124
    Minestrone, 57
    Mushrooms in Lemon Marinade, 68, 76
    Mutabbel (eggplant), 135
    Pork Chops Pizzaiola, 91
    Pork Fajitas with Pan Roasted Peppers, 121
    Ratatouille, 74
    Ratatouille with Chicken Sausage, 110
    Salad, Grilled Eggplant, 43
    Salad, Moroccan Carrot, 41
    Salad, Tomato and Sweet Pepper, 40
    Salad, Tomato and Zucchini, 39
    Sauce, Basic Marinara, 131
    Sauce, Chicken in Red Wine, 112
    Sauce, Roasted Red Pepper Tomato, 128
    Shrimp, Charcoal-Broiled, 95
    Shrimp, South of the Border, 102
    Shrimp, Stir-Fried Pea Shoots and Shiitakes
        with, 93
    Shrimp in New Orleans Sauce, 101
    Shrimp Scampi, Light, 86, 98
    Soup, Broccoli, 63
    Soup, Chicken Florentine, 64
    Soup, Cucumber Mint, 61
    Soup, Lentil Spinach, 58
    Soup, Mom's Garbage, 49, 65–66
    Soup, Southwest Shrimp, 55
    Soup, Spicy Red Pepper, 47, 53
    Soup with Roasted Peppers, Tomato, 51
    Turkey Chili, 106

Turkey for Pocket Sandwiches, 103
Veal Stew with Tomatoes and Balsamic
    Vinegar, 88
Vegetables, Oven-Baked Mixed, 75
Vegetables with Italian-Style Turkey Sausage,
    Oven Roasted, 104
Vegetarian Chili, 123
Vinaigrette, Yellow Tomatoes in Balsamic, 72
Gas, 11–12
Ginger, 12–13
    Chicken, Oriental Grilled, 111
    Chicken Sausage, Spicy Kale Chowder with,
        54
    Shrimp, Charcoal-Broiled, 95
    Shrimp, Stir-Fried Pea Shoots and Shiitakes
        with, 93
    Shrimp with Thai Lemongrass Marinade,
        Grilled, 97
    Tofu Stew, Spicy, 122
    Yellow Tomatoes in Balsamic Vinaigrette, 72
Ginger root
    Asian Slaw, 44
    Asian Style Foil Fish, 94
Goat cheese
    Omelet, Herbed Asparagus, 30
Gout, 13
Grapefruit, 18, 20
Grapes, 20
Green beans
    Green Beans Provençal, 80
    Grilled Salmon and White Bean Salad, 117
    Haricots Verts with Garlic, 79
Green onions
    Omelet with Summer Vegetables, 28
    Shrimp, South of the Border, 102
    Yellow Tomatoes in Balsamic Vinaigrette, 72
Green pepper
    Chicken Breasts with Peppers, 108
    Chicken with Peppers, 114
    Mixed Bell Peppers, Braised, 83
    Peach Salsa, 125, 130
    Pork Chops Pizzaiola, 91
    Shrimp in New Orleans Sauce, 101
    Turkey Chili, 106
Green tea, 16
Grilling, 4
Gum disease, 11

H

Halibut, 20
Haricot verts (green beans)

Haricots Verts with Garlic, 79
Heart disease, 11–13, 16, 21
Herbs and spices, 9–10
Holy Basil, 13
Home remedy tips, 147–48
Horseradish, 13
Hot chilies, 18
Hot flashes, 14
Hot pepper sauce
    South of the Border Shrimp, 102
Hot peppers, 13
Hull, 4

I

Ice cream
    Apple Pie à la Mode Parfaits, 145
Immune system, 12, 22
Impotence, 13
Indigestion, 13
Insomnia, 11, 13, 18
Intestinal gas, 12
Iron, 11, 16
Irritable bowel syndrome, 14

J

Jalapeno pepper
    Mutabbel (eggplant), 135
    Peach Salsa, 125, 130
    Pork Fajitas with Pan Roasted Peppers, 121
    Shrimp with Thai Lemongrass Marinade,
        Grilled, 97
    Soup, Southwest Shrimp, 55
    Soup, Spicy Red Pepper, 47, 53
    Yellow Tomatoes in Balsamic Vinaigrette, 72
Julienne, 4

K

Kale
    Kale, Stewed Beans with, 70
    Kale Chowder with Chicken Sausage, Spicy,
        54
Kidney stones, 13

L

Lake Trout, 20
Lamb
    Lamb and Eggplant, Casserole of, 89
    Lamb Chops, Herb-Marinated, 118
    Lamb with Tarragon, Boneless Loin of, 90
Leek
    Frittata, Asparagus and Leek, 29

Soup, Mom's Garbage, 49, 65–66
Soup, Spicy Red Pepper, 47, 53
Lemon
    Chocolate Glazed Pears, 143
    Moroccan Carrot Salad, 41
    Stewed Beans with Kale, 70
Lemon juice, 13
    Apple Pie à la Mode Parfaits, 145
    Eggplant and Garlic Dip, 126, 134
    Garbanzos with Spinach, 84
    Gazpacho, 60
    Green Beans Provençal, 80
    Mushrooms in Lemon Marinade, 68, 76
    Omelet, Deviled Crab Egg White, 26
    Relish, Black Bean Confetti, 132
    Salad, Moroccan Carrot, 41
    Salad, Tomato and Sweet Pepper, 40
    Salmon and White Bean Salad, Grilled, 117
    Sauce, Poached Salmon with Cucumber, 99
    Sauce, Roasted Red Pepper Tomato, 128
    Shrimp, Charcoal-Broiled, 95
    Soup, Cucumber Mint, 61
    Soup, Sweet Pepper, 52
Lemon zest
    Mutabbel (eggplant), 135
    Omelet, Deviled Crab Egg White, 26
    Salmon and White Bean Salad, Grilled, 117
    Skirt Steak, Marinated, 119
    Trout, Poached, 100
Lemongrass
    Shrimp with Thai Lemongrass Marinade,
        Grilled, 97
Lentils
    Soup, Lentil Spinach, 58
    Soup, Mom's Garbage, 49, 65–66
Lime
    Pork Fajitas with Pan Roasted Peppers, 121
    Salad, Heirloom Tomato, Lime and Onion, 42
    Shrimp Soup, Southwest, 55
    Shrimp with Thai Lemongrass Marinade,
        Grilled, 97
Lime juice
    Asian Slaw, 44
    Baked Chicken with Wild Rice, 109
    Fresh Mango Salsa, 129
    Heirloom Tomato, Lime and Onion Salad, 42
    Peach Salsa, 125, 130
    South of the Border Shrimp, 102
    Tequila Marinated Beef for Fajitas, 115
Liquid measurements, 8
Low-fat protein, 18

Low sodium beans, 9
Lutein, 15–16
Lycopene, 15–16

M
Magnesium, 15–16, 18, 21
Main course
    Beef Burgers, Italian-Style, 120
    Beef for Fajitas, Tequila Marinated, 115
    Beef with Lebanese Spices, Ground, 116
    Chicken, Oriental Grilled, 111
    Chicken and Herbs, Basic Sauté of, 107
    Chicken Breasts with Peppers, 108
    Chicken in Red Wine Sauce, 112
    Chicken Pesto, 113
    Chicken Sausage, Ratatouille with, 110
    Chicken with Peppers, 114
    Chicken with Wild Rice, Baked, 109
    Chili, Vegetarian, 123
    Chili-1 skillet meal, Quick Italian, 105
    Fish, Asian Style Foil, 94
    Fish Fillets in Foil, 85, 96
    Lamb and Eggplant, Casserole of, 89
    Lamb Chops, Herb-Marinated, 118
    Lamb with Tarragon, Boneless Loin of, 90
    Meatballs, Lean, 124
    Pork Chops Pizzaiola, 91
    Pork Fajitas with Pan Roasted Peppers, 121
    Pork Medallions with Herb Marinade, Grilled,
        92
    Salmon and White Bean Salad, Grilled, 117
    Salmon with Cucumber Sauce, Poached, 99
    Shrimp, Charcoal-Broiled, 95
    Shrimp, South of the Border, 102
    Shrimp in New Orleans Sauce, 101
    Shrimp Scampi, Light, 86, 98
    Shrimp Stir-Fried Pea Shoots and Shiitakes
        with, 93
    Shrimp with Thai Lemongrass Marinade,
        Grilled, 97
    Skirt Steak, Marinated, 119
    Tofu Stew, Spicy, 122
    Trout, Poached, 100
    Turkey Chili, 106
    Turkey for Pocket Sandwiches, 103
    Turkey Sausage, Oven Roasted Vegetables
        with Italian-Style, 104
    Veal Stew with Tomatoes and Balsamic
        Vinegar, 88
Male infertility, 13
Manganese, 16, 21

Mango
    Fruit Salad, Summer, 144
    Mango Salsa, Fresh, 129
    Power Muffins, 33
Marinate, 4
Marjoram
    Spicy Red Pepper Soup, 47, 53
Melons, 20
Menopausal symptoms, 16
Menstrual cramps, 11
Mental focus, 12
Metabolism, 11
Microwaving, 4
Minerals, 15
Mint leaf
    Asian Slaw, 44
    Cucumber Mint Soup, 61
    Eggplant Salad, Grilled, 43
    Peaches and Strawberries, Broiled, 141
    Tomatoes with Watermelon, Cherry, 35, 45
    Zucchini and Carrots with Fresh Mint or
        Parsley, 67, 71
Mixed berries
    Summer Fruit Salad, 144
Monounsaturated fats, 15
Monsaturated fat, 15
Mood boosting foods, 18–19
Morning sickness, 12
Mouthwash, 11
Muscles, 11–13
Mushrooms, 10
    Burritos, Egg, Mushroom & Roasted Red
        Pepper, 23, 27
    Chicken in Red Wine Sauce, 112
    Chili-1 skillet meal, Quick Italian, 105
    Fish, Asian Style Foil, 94
    Fish Fillets in Foil, 85, 96
    Mixed Vegetables, Oven-Baked, 75
    Mushrooms in Lemon Marinade, 68, 76
    Pork Chops Pizzaiola, 91
    Quiche, Vegetable Breakfast, 31–32
    Ratatouille, 74
    Shiitakes with Shrimp, Stir-Fried Pea Shoots
        and, 93
    Soup, Hot and Sour, 59
    Soup, Mom's Garbage, 49, 65–66
    Stock, Wild Mushroom, 50
Mustard, 13
    Onion Soup, 56

N
Nausea, 12–13
Navel oranges, 20
Nectarine
    Fruit Salad, Summer, 144
Nectarines, 20
Nerve function, 21
Nutmeg, 9, 13
    Vegetable Breakfast Quiche, 31–32
Nuts, 9

O
Oat bran
    Power Muffins, 33
Oatmeal, 16
    Apple Brown Betty, 137, 139–40
    Apple Pie à la Mode Parfaits, 145
    Outrageous Oatmeal, 24, 34
Olive oil
    Black Bean Confetti Relish, 132
    Cherry Tomatoes with Watermelon, 35, 45
    Gazpacho, 60
    Lamb Chops, Herb-Marinated, 118
    Mutabbel (eggplant), 135
    Pepper Sauté, Italian, 78
    Pork Medallions with Herb, Marinade,
        Grilled, 92
    Quiche, Vegetable Breakfast, 31–32
    Salad, Grilled Eggplant, 43
    Salad, Moroccan Carrot, 41
    Salad, Tomato and Sweet Pepper, 40
    Salad, Tomato and Zucchini, 39
    Salad, Watercress and Orange, 36, 38
    Salmon and White Bean Salad, Grilled, 117
    Veal Stew with Tomatoes and Balsamic
        Vinegar, 88
Omega-3 fatty acids, 16
Onion
    Basic Marinara Sauce, 131
    Caramelized-Onion Sauce, 133
    Chicken with Peppers, 114
    Chili, Turkey, 106
    Chili-1 skillet meal Quick Italian, 105
    Compuesta Dip, 136
    Fish Fillets in Foil, 85, 96
    Fresh Mango Salsa, 129
    Garbanzos with Spinach, 84
    Gazpacho, 60
    Green Beans Provençal, 80
    Lamb and Eggplant, Casserole of, 89
    Lean Meatballs, 124

Mixed Bell Peppers, Braised, 83
Oven-Baked Mixed Vegetables, 75
Peach Salsa, 125, 130
Pepper Sauté, Italian, 78
Quiche, Vegetable Breakfast, 31–32
Ratatouille, 74
Salad, Heirloom Tomato, Lime and Onion, 42
Salad, Tofu, 46
Salad, Watercress and Orange, 36, 38
Salmon and White Bean Salad, Grilled, 117
Shrimp in New Orleans Sauce, 101
Soup, Broccoli, 63
Soup, Chicken Florentine, 64
Soup, Cold Cream of Cucumber, 48, 62
Soup, Lentil Spinach, 58
Soup, Mom's Garbage, 49, 65–66
Soup, Onion, 56
Soup, Spicy Red Pepper, 47, 53
Soup, Sweet Pepper, 52
Soup with Roasted Peppers, Tomato, 51
South of the Border Shrimp, 102
Tequila Marinated Beef for Fajitas, 115
Turkey for Pocket Sandwiches, 103
Veal Stew with Tomatoes and Balsamic
    Vinegar, 88
Orange, 18, 20
Summer Fruit Salad, 144
Watercress and Orange Salad, 36, 38
Orange juice
Baked Chicken with Wild Rice, 109
Orange pepper
Braised Mixed Bell Peppers, 83
Pepper Sauté, Italian, 78
Sweet Pepper Soup, 52
Oregano, 9
Chicken Florentine Soup, 64
Chicken Pesto, 113
Chicken with Peppers, 114
Chili-1 skillet meal, Quick Italian, 105
Italian-Style Beef Burgers, 120
Meatballs, Lean, 124
Minestrone, 57
Mixed Bell Peppers, Braised, 83
Mixed Vegetables, Oven-Baked, 75
Pork Chops Pizzaiola, 91
Ratatouille, 74
Shrimp Scampi, Light, 86, 98
Tequila Marinated Beef for Fajitas, 115
Turkey for Pocket Sandwiches, 103

P
Pan-broil, 4
Pancreas, 12
Pantry list, 9–10
Paprika, 9
    Yellow Tomatoes in Balsamic Vinaigrette, 72
Parasites, 12
Parboil, 4
Pare, 5
Parmesan cheese. *See also* cheese
Beef Burgers, Italian-Style, 120
Lamb and Eggplant, Casserole of, 89
Lentil Spinach Soup, 58
Minestrone, 57
Omelet with Summer Vegetables, 28
Ratatouille, 74
Tomato Soup with Roasted Peppers, 51
Vegetable Breakfast Quiche, 31–32
Vegetables with Italian-Style Turkey Sausage,
    Oven Roasted, 104
Parsley, 12–13
Asparagus and Leek Frittata, 29
Beef with Lebanese Spices, Ground, 116
Cherry Tomatoes with Garlic and Parsley, 81
Chicken Breasts with Peppers, 108
Chicken Florentine Soup, 64
Chicken in Red Wine Sauce, 112
Chicken Pesto, 113
Chicken with Wild Rice, Baked, 109
Eggplant and Garlic Dip, 126, 134
Eggplant Salad, Grilled, 43
Garbanzos with Spinach, 84
Gazpacho, 60
Meatballs, Lean, 124
Mixed Vegetables, Oven-Baked, 75
Mushrooms in Lemon Marinade, 68, 76
Quiche, Vegetable Breakfast, 31–32
Ratatouille, 74
Ratatouille with Chicken Sausage, 110
Salad, Moroccan Carrot, 41
Salad, Tomato and Sweet Pepper, 40
Salad, Tomato and Zucchini, 39
Shrimp, Charcoal-Broiled, 95
Shrimp in New Orleans Sauce, 101
Shrimp Scampi, Light, 86, 98
Soup, Lentil Spinach, 58
Soup, Mom's Garbage, 49, 65–66
Soup, Spicy Red Pepper, 47, 53
Stock, Wild Mushroom, 50
Zucchini and Carrots with Fresh Mint or
    Parsley, 67, 71

Parsnips
    Mom's Garbage Soup, 49, 65–66
Peach, 20
    Broiled Peaches and Strawberries, 141
    Peach Salsa, 125, 130
Pears, 20
    Chocolate Glazed Pears, 143
Peas
    Mom's Garbage Soup, 49, 65–66
Pepper, 13
Pepperment, 13–14
Phosphorus, 21
Pine nuts
    Italian-Style Beef Burgers, 120
Pinto beans
    Southwest Shrimp Soup, 55
Plums, 20
Poach, 5
Pomegranates, 16
Pork
    Pork Chops Pizzaiola, 91
    Pork Fajitas with Pan Roasted Peppers, 121
    Pork Medallions with Herb Marinade, Grilled, 92
Potassium, 15–16, 21
Potatoes
    Vegetable Breakfast Quiche, 31–32
Pound, 5
Preheat, 5
Protein, 16–17, 19, 21
Protein powder
    Outrageous Oatmeal, 24, 34

R
Raisins
    Apple Brown Betty, 137, 139–40
    Power Muffins, 33
Raspberries, 20
Red bell pepper
    Asian Slaw, 44
    Black Bean Confetti Relish, 132
    Egg, Mushroom & Roasted Red Pepper
        Burritos, 23, 27
    Oven-Baked Mixed Vegetables, 75
    Peach Salsa, 125, 130
    Pork Fajitas with Pan Roasted Peppers, 121
    Ratatouille with Chicken Sausage, 110
    Roasted Red Pepper Tomato Sauce, 128
    Roasted Red Peppers, 73
    Tofu Salad, 46
    Tomato Soup with Roasted Peppers, 51

Red chili
    Asian Slaw, 44
    Omelet, Deviled Crab Egg White, 26
Red pepper
    Chicken Breasts with Peppers, 108
    Chicken with Peppers, 114
    Chili, Turkey, 106
    Chili, Vegetarian, 123
    Chili-1 skillet meal, Quick Italian, 105
    Fish Fillets in Foil, 85, 96
    Garbanzos with Spinach, 84
    Gazpacho, 60
    Lamb and Eggplant, Casserole of, 89
    Minestrone, 57
    Mixed Bell Peppers, Braised, 83
    Pepper Sauté, Italian, 78
    Pork Chops Pizzaiola, 91
    Ratatouille, 74
    Salad, Tomato and Sweet Pepper, 40
    Shrimp in New Orleans Sauce, 101
    Soup, Spicy Red Pepper, 47, 53
    Soup, Sweet Pepper, 52
    Stewed Beans with Kale, 70
    Turkey for Pocket Sandwiches, 103
Red pepper flakes, 9
    Chicken, Oriental Grilled, 111
    Chicken with Wild Rice, Baked, 109
    Chili-1 skillet meal Quick Italian, 105
    Fish Fillets in Foil, 85, 96
    Marinara Sauce, Basic, 131
    Ratatouille with Chicken Sausage, 110
    Shrimp, Charcoal-Broiled, 95
    Shrimp Scampi, Light, 86, 98
Red peppercorns
    Cherry Tomatoes with Watermelon, 35, 45
Red Snapper, 20
Red wine
    Marinated Zucchini, 77
    Pepper Sauté, Italian, 78
    Sauce, Caramelized-Onion, 133
    Sauce, Chicken in Red Wine, 112
Red wine vinegar
    Gazpacho, 60
    Mixed Vegetables, Oven-Baked, 75
    Pork Medallions with Herb Marinade, Grilled, 92
    Salad, Grilled Eggplant, 43
    Salad, Tofu, 46
    Salad, Tomato and Zucchini, 39
    Salad, Watercress and Orange, 36, 38
    Soup, Lentil Spinach, 58

Turkey for Pocket Sandwiches, 103
Vegetarian Chili, 123
Reduce, 5
Respiratory complaints, 13–14
Rheumatism, 12
Riboflavin (B2), 21
Rice vinegar
Asian Slaw, 44
Oriental Grilled Chicken, 111
Rice wine
Hot and Sour Soup, 59
Stir-Fried Pea Shoots and Shiitakes with
Shrimp, 93
Roasting, 5
Rosemary, 9, 14
Chicken and Herbs, Basic Sauté of, 107
Lamb Chops, Herb-Marinated, 118
Pork Medallions with Herb Marinade, Grilled,
92
Salmon and White Bean Salad, Grilled, 117
Trout, Poached, 100
Veal Stew with Tomatoes and Balsamic
Vinegar, 88

S
Saffron, 9
Garbanzos with Spinach, 84
Sage, 9, 14
Chicken and Herbs, Basic Sauté of, 107
Salmon and White Bean Salad, Grilled, 117
Spicy Red Pepper Soup, 47, 53
Salads
Asian Slaw, 44
Cherry Tomatoes with Watermelon, 35, 45
Grilled Eggplant Salad, 43
Heirloom Tomato, Lime and Onion Salad, 42
Moroccan Carrot Salad, 41
Tofu Salad, 46
Tomato and Sweet Pepper Salad, 40
Tomato and Zucchini Salad, 39
Watercress and Orange Salad, 36, 38
Salmon, 20
Salmon and White Bean Salad, Grilled, 117
Salmon with Cucumber Sauce, Poached, 99
Salsas. See sauces, dips and salsas
Sauces, dips and salsas
Dip, Compuesta, 136
Dip, Eggplant and Garlic, 126, 134
Mutabbel (eggplant), 135
Relish, Black Bean Confetti, 132
Salsa, Fresh Mango, 129

Salsa, Peach, 125, 130
Sauce, Basic Marinara, 131
Sauce, Caramelized-Onion, 133
Sauce, Roasted Red Pepper Tomato, 128
Sautéing, 5
Scallion
Asian Slaw, 44
Asian Style Foil Fish, 94
Gazpacho, 60
Omelet, Deviled Crab Egg White, 26
Omelet, Herbed Asparagus, 30
Soup, Hot and Sour, 59
Spicy Tofu Stew, 122
Vegetarian Chili, 123
Sea Scallops, 20
Sea trout, 20
Seafood, 18
Sear, 5
Selenium, 18, 22
Sesame oil
Chicken, Oriental Grilled, 111
Fish, Asian Style Foil, 94
Shrimp, Stir-Fried Pea Shoots and Shiitakes
with, 93
Soup, Hot and Sour, 59
Tofu Salad, 46
Tofu Stew Spicy, 122
Sesame seeds, 16
Oriental Grilled Chicken, 111
Shallot
Beans with Kale, Stewed, 70
Black Bean Confetti Relish, 132
Chicken and Herbs, Basic Sauté of, 107
Chicken in Red Wine Sauce, 112
Lamb with Tarragon, Boneless Loin of, 90
Shrimp with Thai Lemongrass Marinade,
Grilled, 97
Sherry
Garbanzos with Spinach, 84
Hot and Sour Soup, 59
Short ribs
Mom's Garbage Soup, 49, 65–66
Shrimp
Omelet, Deviled Crab Egg White, 26
Shrimp, Charcoal-Broiled, 95
Shrimp, South of the Border, 102
Shrimp, Stir-Fried Pea Shoots and Shiitakes
with, 93
Shrimp in New Orleans Sauce, 101
Shrimp Scampi, Light, 86, 98
Shrimp Soup, Southwest, 55

Shrimp with Thai Lemongrass Marinade, Grilled, 97
Side dishes
  Beans with Kale, Stewed, 70
  Garbanzos with Spinach, 84
  Green Beans Provençal, 80
  Haricots Verts with Garlic, 79
  Mixed Bell Peppers, Braised, 83
  Mixed Vegetables, Oven-Baked, 75
  Mushrooms in Lemon Marinade, 68, 76
  Pepper Sauté, Italian, 78
  Ratatouille, 74
  Red Peppers, Roasted, 73
  Tomatoes, Broiled, 82
  Tomatoes in Balsamic Vinaigrette, Yellow, 72
  Tomatoes with Garlic and Parsley, Cherry, 81
  Zucchini, Marinated, 77
  Zucchini and Carrots with Fresh Mint or Parsley, 67, 71
Simmering, 4
Skirt steak
  Marinated Skirt Steak, 119
  Tequila Marinated Beef for Fajitas, 115
Snow peas
  Stir-Fried Pea Shoots and Shiitakes with Shrimp, 93
Sodium, 18
Sore throat, 12, 14
Soups
  Broccoli Soup, 63
  Chicken Florentine Soup, 64
  Chowder with Chicken Sausage, Spicy Kale, 54
  Cold Cream of Cucumber Soup, 48, 62
  Cucumber Mint Soup, 61
  Gazpacho, 60
  Hot and Sour Soup, 59
  Lentil Spinach Soup, 58
  Minestrone, 57
  Mom's Garbage Soup, 49, 65–66
  Onion Soup, 56
  Southwest Shrimp Soup, 55
  Spicy Red Pepper Soup, 47, 53
  Sweet Pepper Soup, 52
  Tomato Soup with Roasted Peppers, 51
  Wild Mushroom Stock, 50
Sour cream
  Chocolate Cheesecake, 142
  Quiche, Vegetable Breakfast, 31–32
  Salmon with Cucumber Sauce, Poached, 99
  Shrimp Soup, Southwest, 55

Sweet Pepper Soup, 52
Soy sauce
  Fish, Asian Style Foil, 94
  Shrimp with Thai Lemongrass Marinade, Grilled, 97
  Soup, Hot and Sour, 59
  Soup, Onion, 56
  Tofu Stew, Spicy, 122
Spaghetti sauce
  Quick Italian Chili-1 skillet meal, 105
Spices and herbs, 9–10
Spinach, 16
  Chicken Florentine Soup, 64
  Garbanzos with Spinach, 84
  Lentil Spinach Soup, 58
  Minestrone, 57
Splenda
  Apple Pie à la Mode Parfaits, 145
  Grilled Shrimp with Thai Lemongrass Marinade, 97
Steaming, 5
Stevia
  Apple Brown Betty, 140
  Asian Slaw, 44
  Beans with Kale, Stewed, 70
  Chocolate Cheesecake, 142
  Chocolate Glazed Pears, 143
  Peaches and Strawberries, Broiled, 141
  Power Muffins, 33
  Yellow Tomatoes in Balsamic Vinaigrette, 72
Stir frying, 5
Stock
  Wild Mushroom Stock, 50
Stomach disorders, 11
Strawberries, 20
  Broiled Peaches and Strawberries, 141
Stress, 13, 18
String beans
  Mom's Garbage Soup, 49, 65–66
Striped Bass, 20
Sun-dried tomatoes, 10
Sweaty palms, 14
Sweet potatoes, 16

T
Tahini
  Mutabbel (eggplant), 135
Tamari
  Tofu Salad, 46
Tarragon, 9
  Boneless Loin of Lamb with Tarragon, 90

Tension headache, 14
Tequila
    Tequila Marinated Beef for Fajitas, 115
Thai chilies
    Shrimp with Thai Lemongrass Marinade,
        Grilled, 97
    Tofu Stew, Spicy, 122
Thyme, 9, 14
Thyme
    Chicken and Herbs, Basic Sauté of, 107
    Chicken in Red Wine Sauce, 112
    Chicken Pesto, 113
    Fish Fillets in Foil, 85, 96
    Lamb Chops, Herb-Marinated, 118
    Shrimp, Charcoal-Broiled, 95
    Soup, Onion, 56
    Soup, Spicy Red Pepper, 47, 53
    Turkey for Pocket Sandwiches, 103
Tobasco sauce, 11
    Shrimp, Stir-Fried Pea Shoots and Shiitakes
        with, 93
    Shrimp in New Orleans Sauce, 101
    Turkey Chili, 106
Tofu
    Chili, Vegetarian, 123
    Soup, Hot and Sour, 59
    Tofu Salad, 46
    Tofu Stew, Spicy, 122
Tomatoes, 10, 16, 20
    Balsamic Vinaigrette, Yellow Tomatoes in, 72
    Beans with Kale, Stewed, 70
    Black Bean Confetti Relish, 132
    Chicken Sausage, Spicy Kale Chowder w, 54
    Chicken with Wild Rice, Baked, 109
    Chili, Turkey, 106
    Chili, Vegetarian, 123
    Dip, Compuesta, 136
    Fish Fillets in Foil, 85, 96
    Gazpacho, 60
    Green Beans Provençal, 80
    Lamb and Eggplant, Casserole of, 89
    Minestrone, 57
    Mixed Bell Peppers, Braised, 83
    Pepper Sauté, Italian, 78
    Pork Chops Pizzaiola, 91
    Quiche, Vegetable Breakfast, 31–32
    Ratatouille, 74
    Ratatouille with Chicken Sausage, 110
    Salad, Tomato and Sweet Pepper, 40
    Salad, Tomato and Zucchini, 39
    Salmon and White Bean Salad, Grilled, 117

Salsa, Fresh Mango, 129
Sauce, Basic Marinara, 131
Sauce, Roasted Red Pepper Tomato, 128
Shrimp in New Orleans Sauce, 101
Soup, Chicken Florentine, 64
Soup, Lentil Spinach, 58
Soup, Mom's Garbage, 49, 65–66
Soup, Southwest Shrimp, 55
Soup, Spicy Red Pepper, 47, 53
Tomato, Lime and Onion Salad, Heirloom, 42
Tomato Soup with Roasted Peppers, 51
Tomatoes, Broiled, 82
Tomatoes with Garlic and Parsley, Cherry, 81
Tomatoes with Watermelon, Cherry, 35, 45
Veal Stew with Tomatoes and Balsamic
        Vinegar, 88
Vegetables with Italian-Style Turkey Sausage,
        Oven Roasted, 104
Tooth decay, 11
Toothache, 11, 13
Tortillas
    Burritos, Egg, Mushroom & Roasted Red
        Pepper, 23, 27
    Pork Fajitas with Pan Roasted Peppers, 121
Trout, 20
    Poached Trout, 100
Tumeric, 9, 14
    Yellow Tomatoes in Balsamic Vinaigrette, 72
Turkey, 18
    Beef with Lebanese Spices, Ground, 116
    Chicken Sausage, Spicy Kale Chowder with,
        54
    Chili-1 skillet meal, Quick Italian, 105
    Meatballs, Lean, 124
    Turkey Chili, 106
    Turkey for Pocket Sandwiches, 103
    Turkey Sausage, Oven Roasted Vegetables
        with Italian-Style, 104
Turkey broth
    Chicken Sausage, Spicy Kale Chowder with,
        54
Turnips
    Mom's Garbage Soup, 49, 65–66
Tyrosine, 18

U
Urinary tract infection, 11

V
Vanilla
    Power Muffins, 33

Veal
  Veal Stew with Tomatoes and Balsamic
    Vinegar, 88
Veal stock
  Veal Stew with Tomatoes and Balsamic
    Vinegar, 88
Vegetable broth
  Mom's Garbage Soup, 49, 65–66
  Stewed Beans with Kale, 70
Vegetable stock
  Sweet Pepper Soup, 52
Vegetables, 4–5, 20
Vitamin A, 16, 22
Vitamin B2, 21
Vitamin B12, 22
Vitamin B-complex, 17, 21
Vitamin C, 11, 15–16, 18, 22
Vitamin D, 17, 21
Vitamin E, 15–16, 22
Vitamin K, 15–16, 22

W
Walnuts, 16
  Power Muffins, 33
Water, 19
Watercress
  Watercress and Orange Salad, 36, 38
Watermelon
  Cherry Tomatoes with Watermelon, 35, 45
Weight loss, 16
Wheat bran
  Power Muffins, 33
Wheat germ
  Power Muffins, 33
White beans
  Grilled Salmon and White Bean Salad, 117
White rice vinegar
  Spicy Tofu Stew, 122
White vinegar
  Ratatouille, 74
White wine
  Chicken and Herbs, Basic Sauté of, 107
  Chicken Breasts with Peppers, 108
  Green Beans Provençal, 80
  Lamb with Tarragon, Boneless Loin of, 90
  Pork Chops Pizzaiola, 91
  Soup, Onion, 56
  Trout, Poached, 100
White wine vinegar
  Poached Salmon with Cucumber Sauce, 99
Whole-grain bread, 19

Wild rice
  Baked Chicken with Wild Rice, 109
Wild salmon, 16–17

Y
Yellow bell pepper
  Black Bean Confetti Relish, 132
  Ratatouille with Chicken Sausage, 110
Yellow pepper
  Mixed Bell Peppers, Braised, 83
  Pepper Sauté, Italian, 78
  Pepper Soup, Sweet, 52
  Turkey for Pocket Sandwiches, 103
Yogurt, 17
  Dip, Compuesta, 136
  Dip, Eggplant and Garlic, 126, 134
  Power Muffins, 33
  Salmon with Cucumber Sauce, Poached, 99
  Soup, Cucumber Mint, 61
  Soup, Sweet Pepper, 52

Z
Zinc, 22
Zucchini
  Omelet with Summer Vegetables, 28
  Ratatouille, 74
  Vegetables with Italian-Style Turkey Sausage,
    Oven Roasted, 104
  Zucchini, Marinated, 77
  Zucchini and Carrots with Fresh Mint or
    Parsley, 67, 71
  Zucchini Salad, Tomato and, 39

Made in the USA
Lexington, KY
09 December 2009